CASE STUDY METHOD
THEORY AND PRACTICE
Research and Management Approaches

CASE STUDY METHOD
THEORY AND PRACTICE
Research and Management Approaches

A. Mustafa

ATLANTIC
PUBLISHERS & DISTRIBUTORS (P) LTD

Published by

ATLANTIC

PUBLISHERS & DISTRIBUTORS (P) LTD

7/22, Ansari Road, Darya Ganj,
New Delhi-110002
Phones : +91-11-23273880, 23275880, 23280451
Fax : +91-11-23285873
Web : www.atlanticbooks.com
E-mail : info@atlanticbooks.com

Branch Office
5, Nallathambi Street, Wallajah Road,
Chennai-600002
Phones : +91-44-64611085, 32413319
E-mail : chennai@atlanticbooks.com

ISBN 978-81-269-1006-9

Printed in India at Nice Printing Press, A-33/3A, Site-IV, Industrial Area, Sahibabad, Ghaziabad, U.P.

Foreword

I am very much pleased to write the foreword for this book. There are a few books on case study. But there is no book which gives solution to cases. Of course, there is no 'the' answer for any given case. Solution/answer may differ from case to case, from time to time, from person to person, from situation to situation, and from place to place. Dr. A. Mustafa, Principal, Syed Hameedha Arts and Science College, Kilakarai, Tamil Nadu, one of the 14 sponsored institutions of Mohamed Sathak Trust, has given alternative solutions for a given case. This book provides an overall picture of different aspects of case study besides outlining the processes of approaching and writing a case.

I hope the students of B.B.A., M.B.A., and M.S. (IT&M) courses can make use of this book confidently and widen their theoretical and practical knowledge about case study.

T.R. Gurumoorthy
Professor
Department of International
Business and Commerce
Alagappa University
Karaikudi-630 004
Tamil Nadu

Preface

A case study is a comprehensive study of a social unit—person, group, institution, district or community. Each situation—whether it is an entire lifecycle or a particular process of that cycle—forms part of a case study in which the dependent factors act as situations. The method that we apply to gather facts regarding the interrelated factors by which we describe the social processes or sequences of events, or by which we study the individual behaviour in its social setting, or by which we analyse and compare cases leading to generalisations or formulation of principles is known as the case study method. The essence of this method is that it derives its substance and patterns from actual situations and not from any preconceived notions.

There are several types of case studies—single, deviant, comparative or multiple—each following certain assumptions like totality of being, underlying unity, complexity of social phenomena, influence of time, etc. The unit under study is considered representative of the total, believing that it carries all the major characteristics of the group.

The case study method is widely used these days in management and entrepreneurship as it serves various objectives, like putting textbook knowledge about management into practice, diagnosing problems, analysing and evaluating alternatives, making workable plans of action, and providing exposure to a range of managerial situations, thus offering a basis for useful comparisons. In a sense, cases are laboratory materials which offer a reasonable substitute for actual experience by bringing a variety of management problems and opportunities.

Case Study Method: Theory and Practice is a pioneer attempt to present various aspects related to case study method such as types, characteristics, basic assumptions, objectives, advantages, limitations, procedures, etc. The book also provides guidelines to make a good presentation of case, analytical tools for case study, and techniques for oral presentation, group discussion and industry analysis. It also contains some important case studies to enrich the reader's experience about various situations.

This book will be highly useful to the students of BBA, BBM, MBA and research scholars in the field of management.

A. Mustafa

Contents

PART B
CASE STUDY—A GUIDE TO ANALYSIS

PART C
CASE STUDY—HOW TO ARRIVE AT A SOLUTION —A PRACTICAL APPROACH

PART A

CASE STUDY—AN INTRODUCTION

Case Study—An Introduction

WHAT IS A CASE?

A case is a written description of an organisation (or any of its parts) covering all or some of its aspects for a certain period of time. It sets forth the events and organisational circumstances surrounding a particular managerial situation. Most cases contain information about the organisation's history, its internal operations and its external environment. Though there is no standard order of presentation, many cases include information about the industry, the competitive conditions, the products and markets, the physical facilities, the work climate, the skills and personality of managers, the organisational structure, together with the financial and quantitative data relating to production, marketing, personnel, and so forth. Cases may relate to profit seeking government or public service organisations.

Despite its known deficiencies, the case method is widely used by universities and professional institutes throughout the world, especially for imparting knowledge and developing skills in the area of corporate strategy or strategic management.

A good case places students in a realistic situation where they can practice making decisions. Though a case may contain plenty of information, in some cases running into several pages, there is no such thing as a truly complete case. Students often say (or complain) that they have too little information in the case. While this may be true, it should be appreciated that, many a time, managers in the real world too have information which can hardly be described as sufficient. In fact, a manager has far less opportunity for study and interaction with others as a student has. The managers cannot afford to delay making decisions until they are satisfied with the quality and quantity of available information. Such a time, perhaps, may never arrive. Like a real world manager, a student of corporate strategy must make a decision, making best use of whatever information is available and making assumptions about whatever is unknown or is not available.

Meaning of Case Study

Case study is often termed a method, a technique, an approach to social reality and a mode of organising data in terms of some chosen units. According to Pauline V. Young, a fairly exhaustive study of a person or group is called a life or case history. In this sense, a comprehensive study of a social unit, be that a person, a group, a social institution, a district or a community, is called a case study.

Thus, each situation, whether it is an entire life cycle or a particular process of this cycle, forms part of a case study and the dependent factors as situations. The method by which we gather facts regarding 'total' situation or combination of interrelated factors by which we describe the social processes or sequences of events or by which we study the individual behaviour in its social setting and by which we analyse and compare cases leading to generalisations or formulation of principles, is known as case study method.

It may be relevant at this juncture to point out the views of Goode and Hatt. They opined that case study is a way of organising social data so as to preserve the unitary character of the social object being studied. Expressed somewhat differently, it is an approach which views any social unit as a whole. This approach includes the development of a unit, which may be a person or a family or other social group, a set of relationships or processes or even an entire culture. Case study is, thus, a technique which considers all pertinent aspects of a situation employing as the unit of study. It tries to understand the interplay of various complex variables and considers the extension of similar logic to the total phenomena.

Definition of Case Study

Case study is a way of organising social data so as to preserve the unitary character of the social object being studied. Expressed somewhat differently it is an approach which views any social unit as a whole.

— *Goode and Hatt*

Case study method may be defined as a small inclusive and intensive study of an individual in which investigator brings to bear all his skills and methods or as a systematic gathering of enough information about a person to permit one to understand how he or she functions as a unit of society.

— *Yang Hsin Pao*

The case study is a form of qualitative analysis involving the very careful and complete observation of a person, a situation or an institution.

— *Biesanz and Biesanz*

Characteristics of Case Study

A case is often described as a 'Chunk' of reality brought into the classroom for dealing, observation, analysis and decision.

The crux of the case method is that it derives its life and patterns from actual situations and not from any pre-conceived notions.

The main focus in any case should be to make the participants work for themselves, carry out the analysis of situations and arrive at their own decisions to be drawn from the material placed before them.

This pre-supposes that the case itself should be such which should give a situation very clearly and should be worthy of serious and useful discussions. The case could be verbal, a letter, a report or even a discussion between two or more people actually recorded. The case should also relate either to a situation in personal background, production background or marketing background or may involve situations of an organisation in its entirety.

A good case should invariably have the following characteristics:

1. It should create interest while reading and, thus, attract attention of the participants.
2. It must give a situation where there is a possibility of differing views. As obvious solution or single solution, case cannot provoke any discussion.
3. Case study is a deep, detailed and intensive study of a social unit.
4. It is a method of qualitative analysis.
5. It is a comprehensive study.
6. It preserves the wholeness of the unit.
7. In case study, all the variables and traits are linked with one another.
8. It aims at studying everything about something, rather than something about everything.
9. Unit of study may be an individual, a family, an institution, a cultural group or an entire community.
10. Case study covers sufficiently wide cycle of time. According to P.V. Young, case data may be gathered exhaustively on the entire life cycle of a social unit or a definite section of it.
11. As the study is more detailed and extends over a wider expanse of time, the number of units has to be small. The number may vary from a single unit to a few dozen or even a few hundred.

Types of Case Study

The case study calls for laborious, painstaking collection and exploration of a variety of original data, if a reliable portrait and the functioning of the subject of study is to be obtained. This is not possible usually for a lone researcher who, thus, limits his study to a few aspects; but any generalisation on such insufficient or incomplete data is hazardous. To avoid the charge of being superficial, he may cover a number of instances to determine whether a particular trait is commonly present or not. This type of narrow case study is seen in opinion poll or population census. However, the case study method involves an intensive search for data to illumine even a single true attribute or characteristic; the exercise usually becomes time consuming and expensive.

In one sense, the case study method is a vertical study. It delves into the past, brings the description up to the present and tries to predict the future. In another sense, it is a horizontal study, seeking to find out and establish the interrelationship between the reference unit and the rest of the social or economic system. The case study, is thus, both a longitudinal and latitudinal study. It has a historical approach and its object is to give a picture of the living throbbing organism that a social unit has. This calls for an interdisciplinary approach. Take for instance, the research on entrepreneurship at Coimbatore. Assume that the researcher has taken the case study of a leading industrialist in that Manchester of the South India. A study of the family status in his childhood, the upbringing, the cultural matrix, etc., needs the help of sociology and psychology also. It calls for a multiplicity of methods and tapping variety of sources, e.g., persons, institutions, interviews, schedules, personal observation, scoring devices, ecological method, records, biographies, etc.

There are different types of case study which are as follows:

(i) Single case study

When a single case is studied in detail, it is known as a single case study. A single case study may be either exploratory, descriptive or explanatory. Sometimes it is used to test a theory.

(ii) Deviant case study

When a case which is totally different from existing theory or knowledge is studied in detail, it is known as a deviant case study. Here, the researcher may look for factors that may explain why the case differs. Research like this may lead to the revision or clarification of existing theories.

(iii) Comparative or multiple case study

Instead of a single case, if the researcher studies about two or more than two cases in detail it may be called comparative case study or multiple case study. Multiple case study enables a researcher to test a single theory more than once. Hence, it has more explanatory power than a single case study. For some cases, similar results will be predicted; for others, different results.

Normal, abnormal, positive and negative case studies are other types.

Informational type case studies

These include a variety of items like working environment, inter-organisational context, co-ordination activities, problem areas, history of events, inhibiting factors on decision-making, etc. This type increases the awareness about the environment, help in the decision-making process. This also helps in evaluation of consequences of decision.

Appraisal cases

This type involves problem-solving and decision-making.

Historical cases

Involving research and educational interests.

Project cases

These are cases with radical educational process involving interactions.

Live and experimental cases or functional cases

Involving social welfare, rehabilitation or introduction of ideas and analytical concepts. These types of cases help in analysing socio/psychic problems like drug addiction, alcoholism, etc.

Whatever be the type of case study, just as a doctor diagnoses the disease by a critical examination and does not go about just by symptoms, one should go about locating the real problem by an in-depth study of the case rather than a surface study of the symptoms and then look in for solutions. There will be certain areas of agreement and some of disagreement. Once we list out these symptoms we would be able to diagnose the real problems and then solutions therefor.

BASIC ASSUMPTIONS

Case study is based upon following basic assumptions:

1. Totality of the being

The first fundamental assumption of case study is that a unit is indivisible whole and cannot be studied piecemeal and in fragments. In order to study the behaviour of an individual at any particular time, it is not enough to study his situation at the particular time alone. We must have his whole life history, his background before we can really explain his behaviour at the particular time. It is because of this basic assumption, that the unit has to be studied in its wholeness.

2. Underlying unity

The other assumption is that, in the face of apparent diversity among different units, there is an underlying unity. A particular unit has its uniqueness but it is not different from other units in all respects. It is also a representative of a group and can be studied as a type, rather than a pure individual. This underlying unity makes it possible for us to apply the inference drawn from the unit or group of units to the group as a whole. It is because of this assumption that the study of a particular unit has some fruitful application in the prediction and control of the social phenomena.

3. Complexity of social phenomena

Social phenomenon is not only a total whole, it is very complex also. A greater part of man's life is subjective, unknown and incapable of observation. The understanding of human nature and his actions, therefore, requires, much deeper probe and a keen insight. A sympathetic study of human behaviour is, thus, possible only through case study.

4. Influence of time

Social phenomena are influenced by time also. In order to find out the real motives behind any action, we have to study the problem in its historical perspective. Without the knowledge of the past history, the study would remain incomplete and would yield results that would be untrue. It is because of this influence of time that, under case study, we examine the unit over full cycle of time.

To sum up:

(i) It is assumed that a unit is representative of the total. It is believed that the unit carries with it major characteristics of the group. For instance, in studying human beings human nature is taken as similar in people, although their conduct may change in certain circumstances.

(ii) It is also assumed that the total phenomena are much complex and the study of which is neither advisable, nor practicable. As such, few cases are considered adequate and useful to study them in detail where project on the interrelationship and factors are involved.

(iii) In case study method the unit is studied as a whole.

(iv) Time factor has its impact on social phenomena. So, a historical perspective is assumed to be present for the study of the problem.

(v) Although much of a person's past may be obscure to him or out of reach to a researcher, it is possible to find in most persons an underlying reaction system. This is termed 'Unity Thema' by Gardner Murphy, which can serve as the fundamental basis for the exploration of personality.

Case Study and Interview

Case study method is similar to qualitative or free story type interview in many respects and the distinction between the two must be made clear at this stage to avoid any misunderstanding. Both the methods consider comparatively few cases and rely on free story type narratives of the life situations, and feeling of the respondent. But, in the case study method number of cases taken is much smaller than the interview method. Information to be gathered in the case study is more comprehensive in nature. Interviews are also held, but they are more prolonged and continue over long periods. Interview is, thus, only one of the methods in case study and besides the interview, other methods such as observations and various types of objective tests are freely used in the case studies. Case study is thus a more comprehensive form of investigation and interview is only a part of its technique.

OBJECTIVES OF CASE METHOD

The objectives of the case method are to:

- help you to acquire the skills of putting textbook knowledge about management into practice. Managers succeed not so much because of what they know but because of what they do.
- get you out of the habit of being a receiver of facts, concepts and techniques and get into the habit of diagnosing problems, analysing and evaluating alternatives, and formulating workable plans of action.
- train you to work out answers and solutions for yourselves, as opposed to relying upon the authoritative crutch of the teacher/counsellor or a textbook.
- provide you exposure to a range of organisations and managerial situations (which might take a lifetime to experience personally), thus offering you a basis for comparison in your working as a career manager.

Reading books, articles and listening to lectures alone cannot develop managerial skills. For most managerial problems, readymade answers do not exist, or, perhaps, cannot exist. Each situation is different, requiring its own diagnosis and evaluation before action can be initiated. Case studies allow *learning by doing* to occur. They stimulate the reality of a managerial situation and a manager's job. In a sense, cases are laboratory materials and offer a reasonable substitute for actual experience by bringing a variety of management problems and opportunities into the classroom.

Students often ask their teacher/counsellor, "What is the right answer/solution?" If the discussion in the class concludes without clear answers or a clear consensus on what actually happened or what should/ought to be done, some students feel frustrated. While in some cases it would be possible for you and the counsellor to develop a consensus, in other cases, it may, perhaps, not be possible. As in real world, hard answers to cases do not exist. Therefore, issues are discussed and various alternatives and approaches are evaluated. Usually a good argument can be made for more than one course of action. The important thing for students to understand in case analysis is that it is the exercise of *identifying, diagnosing and recommending* that counts rather than discovering the "right answer". The essence of case analysis is to become skilled in the process of designing workable action plans through evaluation of the prevailing circumstances.

If case method rests on the principle of learning by doing, it all depends on you as to how much gain you can derive by making your own analysis and reaching your own decisions, and then participating in the classroom in a collective analysis and discussion of the issues. Since a case assignment emphasises student participation, it is obvious that the effectiveness of the class discussion depends upon each student having *studied the case beforehand. A case assignment, therefore, requires conscientious preparative before class.* You cannot expect to get much out of hearing the class discuss a case with which you are unfamiliar or not fully prepared for.

The pedagogical objective of case method is very much different from the usual teaching in the classroom. Instead of the professor/instructor/counsellor, it is the students who do most of the talking. The counsellor/instructor's role is to solicit student participation and guide the discussion. The counsellor might begin by restating the questions given at the end of each case or he might even propose or frame some new questions like: What is the organisation's strategy? What are the strategic issues and problems confronting the company? What is your assessment of the company's situation? Is the industry an attractive one to be in? Is management doing a good job? Are the organisation's objectives and strategies compatible with its skills and resources?

The students are expected to engage in discussion with each other, with the counsellor listening to them patiently and providing direction/guidance as and when required, so that the whole discussion remains on the track. It is the students who carry the main burden of analysing the situation and then presenting main and defending their analysis in the counselling sessions.

You should, therefore, not expect your counsellor to say: "Here is the right answer", etc. Although you should do your "Here is how to do it" own independent work and thinking, you should not hesitate to discuss the case with other students.

Case Research Design

Case research is the most widely used formal research design. It can be carried out in the field such as survey of consumer attitudes toward a new product concept or it may be conducted in a library by the survey of available secondary data. But it is generally used for collecting cases. The collected cases are the typical studies generally used to find three factors:

1. features which are common to all cases in the general groups;
2. features which are not common to all cases, but are common to certain sub-groups; and
3. features which are unique to a specific case.

Case data are usually gathered in the field through either observation or personal interview method. Case data may be presented in either one or a two-dimensional format. Generally, analysis in case design does not use the sophisticated quantitative and statistical techniques. The stress is more on qualitative analysis of collected data.

Conclusions are drawn from comparisons and differences among various points. In some instances, the investigator is more interested in first two groups of above listed factors e.g., those that are common to all in the class and those, that are common to all in a sub-class. In other instances, the latter two groups of factors may be more important i.e., those factors which are common to a sub-group and those factors which are unique to an individual case.

Thus, the case design of research is based on the *specific objectives* of a study and is primarily a question of sampling. If factors common to all items of a group are sought, then a representative group of cases from the universe of buyers might be selected. If it is desired to find what made some salesmen more successful than others, the design might include cases from two abnormal groups—successful salesmen and unsuccessful salesmen.

CASE STUDY AND STATISTICAL METHODS

The distinction between a statistical approach and case study method is succinctly pointed out by Pauline Young: 'Statistical technique depends upon the deduction of data to quantitative terms in order to yield totals, averages and correlations; the case study technique seeks date in terms of processes which, for the most part, cannot be stated numerically. The statistician selects certain specific factors involved in social institutions and manipulates them so as to discover the relations between the several variables. The case student examines single situations, persons, groups, institutions as a complex whole in order to identify types and processes. The statistical technique refers to the period of investigation, which, being dated is an instance of static approach. The case study with its emphasis on the evolution of the unit right from its genesis, is an instance of dynamic approach. Primarily as a depth study, it also investigates into the direct and indirect relationship between the reference unit and its sister, ancillary, and subsidiary units in the entire social set up. It has a micro approach, yet it is capable of filling up the gaps of knowledge about entire system and provide building blocks to undertake a macro analysis.

Case study differs from statistical method in the following respects:

1. Case history depends upon narrative type description of life situations, while statistical method tries to measure them quantitatively. Thus statistical methods are more structured and formal, while the case study has a lot of free scope of description. It is not subjected

to rigid classification and categorisation of information beforehand.

2. Case study takes into consideration comparatively fewer cases and aims at more intensive study. The statistical method, on the other hand, believes in inertia of large numbers. Thus, a sufficiently large number of cases is taken into consideration in order to arrive at valid generalisations.
3. Case studies are intensive in nature. The number of cases is limited but the aspects of life to be studied cover a very wide range. Statistical studies are extensive in nature. They include a large number of cases but study one or two aspects only.
4. Selection of cases in the case study is not based on sampling as in case of statistical methods. The study of cases is so prolonged and thorough that conveniences of study become a major factor in deciding as to what will be studied. Only these few cases are taken up which can be taken as sufficiently representative of the whole group.
5. Case study generalisations are based upon *Common-sense inferences.* They are not subjected to *rigid mathematical treatment* as in case of statistical methods. Case study generalisations are, therefore, thought to be less reliable because of subjectivity in them.
6. Case study method lays a greater stress upon the emotional side of social phenomena. It is based on the assumption that circumstances and the emotional implications conditioned by them have a great influence upon the activities of men or even a group. The life of a man is an integrated whole, *it cannot be studied piecemeal.* Therefore, in order to understand the significance of various actions and reactions, the whole life of subject must be studied in proper sequence, and actual life situations causing them should be given due emphasis. The statistical method, on the other hand, is based on the assumption that if large number

of cases are taken into consideration the study of even stray aspect of life is possible.

Similarity of the Two Methods

L.L. Bernard says, "The real source of methodological error (in case study) is in supposing that statistical generalisation can proceed from case data without some sort of statistical method." He means that the two methods, case study and statistical, are similar and interdependent upon each other. Whatever may be the process of collecting case data, valid generalisation cannot be taken unless it has been subjected to statistical treatment. Kimball Young rightly says, "As a matter of fact many of the basic problems of (case study) method are not unlike those of statistics." He has given the following points of similarity between the two methods:

1. The more careful case studies also recognize the problem of sampling since the aim is to avoid the temptation to generalise from one case.
2. References are frequently made to typical case which, in many respects, is similar to measures of central tendency or averages in statistical terminology.
3. Case study tries to locate the variations in the reactions and activities of the subject. This type of study is fundamentally similar to the statistical measure of variability.
4. The case study data is also compared with other cases to find out the points of similarity and dissimilarity and the generalisations thus drawn are the same as those in the study of statistical correlation or study of covariance.

It is thus, quite clear that fundamentally the two methods are same and interdependent upon each. According to Bernard, "so-called commonsense inferences from cases amount to nothing less than informal statistical generalisation. Formal statistical generalisation are more adequate, when practicable" attempts are being made to make case study methods more precise and accurate by the use of statistical methods and the statistical methods more real and practical by application of case date.

Bain has correctly remarked, "The question today is not case study or quantitative research, it is rather on 'and' relationship."

Advantages of Case Study Method

Although doubts are expressed regarding the representativeness of the case method, it has occupied an important field in social research and is gaining ground now in business research. The chief advantages of this method are as follows:

1. Intensive in nature

Case study method is intensive in nature. It takes up the study of a unit in its entirety. As such, it leaves greater scope for indepth study of particular problem.

2. Aids to study complex problems

Case studies are of particular value when one is seeking help on a problem in which interrelationships of a number of factors are involved, and in which it is difficult to understand the individual factors without considering their relationships with each other. For example, assume that the rate of capacity utilisation of cement factories in Andhra Pradesh is declining. It is better to study a few units to understand as to why it is happening.

3. Comprehensive study

Inferences are obtained from the study of an entire situation; an entity, rather than from the study of one or several selected aspects alone. In case of individuals, it deals with various aspects of one's life from the past to the present of an individual thoroughly.

4. Describes a real event

A case study is a description of a real event or situation, unlike other studies which may involve abstraction from real situations.

5. Helps find deviations

The case study method helps to find out the deviant units which are marginal and are not compared with the amount of information yielded by general cases.

6. More accurate

This method is more accurate, as it obtains comparatively correct data by approaching the unit or units under study. Probably as a result of the longer, more intimate association of the researcher and respondent, it may be possible to go deeper into the issues.

7. Aids sampling

The case method is useful in sampling, because it classifies the units efficiently on the basis of their qualifications or characteristics.

8. Aids questionnaire preparation

It is also useful in making the questionnaire more pointed towards the problem. Indepth study of cases will enable the researcher to gain sufficient understanding of the problem leading to accurate formulation of schedule or questionnaire for the similar studies.

9. It can be used as a cautionary story so that the participants do not repeat the mistakes committed by others (e.g., concept of many safety errors).
10. May be used for arriving at general conclusions on important management principles from specific examples (e.g., concept of delegation).
11. Practicing techniques or applying principles in the risk free environment of a classroom (e.g., making an investment decision based on supplied information).
12. Extending experience by role-playing various parts which often cannot be done in real life (e.g., be able to view a problem from someone else's point of view, say through the eyes of a Finance Manager).

In a developing country like India, there are certain limitations and constraints in using the case study method, although this is an innovative technique in improving managerial skills. There are various problems like lingua franca, socio-political and cultural milieu, religious fervours, shyness of the participants, secrecy in sharing of information, lack of professional skills and non-acceptance of existence of such skills, problems in dissemination of information and dissipation of details.

Case study helps in formulating valid hypothesis. When various cases are thoroughly studied and carefully analysed, the researcher can arrive at various generalisations, which may be developed into useful hypothesis. In fact, study of relevant literature and case study are the only two potent sources of hypotheses.

Case study is useful in framing questionnaire, schedule or other forms. If a questionnaire is drafted after thorough case study, we can know the peculiarities of the group as well individual units, the type of response likely to be available, pet liking and aversions of the people.

Case study is helpful in stratification of the sample. By studying the individual units thoroughly, we can put them in definite classes or types. Thus, it is helpful in perfect stratification of the sample.

It is possible to locate deviant cases. Daviant cases are those units that behave against the proposed hypothesis. A general tendency is to ignore them, but for scientific analysis, they are very important. The analysis of such cases may lead to a lot of clarification of theory itself.

Where the problem under study forms a process rather than one incident, e.g., courtship process, clique formation, etc., case study is the suitable method. The case data is essential for valid study of problems.

Case study enlarges the range of personal experience of the researcher. In statistical method, generally, a narrow range of topic is selected, and the researcher's knowledge is limited to the particular aspect only. In case study, the whole range of subject's life is studied and the range of knowledge is naturally enlarged. The researcher gets an intimate knowledge of many other aspects.

Case study helps to find the significance of the recorded data within the life of individual and later on within the life of the classes of individuals. The researcher comes into contact with different classes of people, a thief, a pick pocket and the like. He watches their life and hears their experiences. Thus, he is able to gain the experiences of even such life which he is never expected to lead.

Thus, we find that case data is of no mean importance in social research. Techniques have now been developed to make it more perfect and remove the chances of bias. For a perfect research the use of both the methods, case history and statistical, are essential. In spite of everything said against it, case study will remain the most fundamental method of study of the social phenomena. It is the basis of all social investigation and would remain so in spite of the development technology of research in social sciences.

Case study discussion encourages managers to develop their own management principles for solving day-to-day problems without being continuously spoon-fed either by the circulars or bye-laws of the management.

While dealing with actual cases, the managers are encouraged to find out solutions instead of going through routine management concepts as fed to them through their rules and regulations and time consuming question-answer correspondence.

Case study discussions arouse keen interest among the managers and they get involved in solving a problem by themselves.

Case study method encourages full participation by the managers as they get themselves actively involved in solving problems.

Case study method develops the ability of analysing the problems, ability of logical thinking and presenting their own view in the context of other views.

Case study method pre-supposes in a way collective thinking, and therefore, develops an ability of patient listening which is a very important requirement in any problem-solving action.

Case discussions do not bring fatigue which is not uncommon while hearing a lecture.

Case study discussions give an opportunity to everyone to hear views of different types of different people and helps in changing attitude gradually that too without arousing resentment as the views are expressed about a case and not a discussion between one and the other.

A participant in a case study in a given case imagines himself in the position of the executive and tries his hand at a solution. The cross examination to which he is subjected to by his colleagues and the comments of the teacher help him to re-examine and improve the solution wherever possible.

The biggest advantage of case study discussion is that, in fact, it serves as an "experience pool" as it utilises an experience of members of the whole group, which invariably encourages cross fertilisation of ideas.

The chief advantages of the case method are: (i) inferences are obtained from the study of an entire situation, an entity rather than from a study of one or several selected aspects alone; (ii) a case study is a historical and microscopic description of a real event or situation, hence, generates more data; and (iii) more accurate data are obtained.

The case method offers students an opportunity to communicate and convince their fellow students and their counsellors of the correctness of their viewpoints. This is analogous to the situation where a manager must persuade others to accomplish organisational purposes. The case analysis and discussion help the students in developing analytical communication and interpersonal skills which are vital for success in management. The method also provides some opportunity to the students to relate their viewpoints with those of the others. While defending his own viewpoint, a student has, also, to develop an appreciation for the viewpoints held by others.

Disadvantages of Case Study Method

Despite the above mentioned utility of the case method, there are certain inherent limitations in the case method. They are mainly centred round the lack of objectivity, expensive nature and the use of sampling methods. A brief description of some of the limitations of the case method is provided hereunder:

1. Lack of objectivity

This lack of objectivity carries over into the analysis of case data, because by definition formal statistical procedures are not used. The analysis is based on the intuition of the investigator. This may lead to unwarranted conclusions.

2. Error in selection of cases

The selection of representative cases is always a problem. More so, the representativeness is a subjective decision based on certain characteristics. For instance, in the analysis of performance of an employee, one may think that education and skill are more important than motivation and commitment. The criteria we use decides the sample cases.

3. Overconfidence

In this type of study, a researcher may become overconfident. Since he studies various aspects of the life of an individual, he may think that he knows everything about human beings. But it is seen very often that many other aspects of life were hidden about which the respondent himself was ignorant.

4. Problems in data collection

Data collection is yet another difficulty in case study method. We may receive exceptionally qualitative information or we may get utterly useless data, depending on the mental disposition of the respondents. For instance, the Mass Interview Programme undertaken as part of the Hawthorne studies led the investigators nowhere, till the interview is directed by them. The employees gave standard and repetitive answers as though there existed a near unanimity in their thinking and approach. Investigators could secure valuable data only when they switched over from 'directed' to 'non-directed' interview technique.

Further, as case studies involve detailed description of complete situations, it is difficult to develop formal methods of observation and recording. Informal methods tend to become subjective than objective and involve mere hope.

5. Too much generalisation

Investigators, out of their confidence, feel that cases they have studied are truly representative of the phenomena and start generalising the conclusions of the sample to the universe. They hardly realise the nature of cases and their representativeness.

6. Qualitative in nature

Case study method is essentially qualitative in nature. It only deals with certain particular or peculiar characteristics of a human being or a group or a unit. Quantification of the results is not possible in this type of study. Statistical methods are inappropriate to case studies.

7. Unorganised

Case studies are generally unorganised and controlling of respondents may not be feasible. Similarly, organisation of historical data also becomes difficult.

8. Costs in time and money

Another limitation of the case method is that it involves huge cost and time. Each case becomes a research in itself and collection of even 100 adequately documented cases may easily consume 2 years of student's time. That is why, research students working in the areas of small industry or 'Entrepreneurship' limit their sample to about 100 or 50 depending on the depth of the issues needed to be studied. Since the data are not usually standardised, the system of keeping records and of developing techniques for standardising the observations must be rather elaborate. Over such a lengthy period, the loss of potential cases from the sample drawn may be very great and resultant costs of tracing such cases may prove to be high.

To sum up: (i) it is difficult to develop formal methods of observation and recording; (ii) lack of objectivity is carried over into the analysis of case data; (iii) it does not lend itself to generalisation due to small sample; and (iv) also it is costly, complex, and superficial in approach.

Limitations

Case study method has often been criticised on the basis of following limitations:

1. The first and the foremost difficulty, the one that is the basis of all other, is the overconfidence that the researcher, develops in his mind. In case of statistical studies, the researcher knows his limitations. He knows that he has studied only one aspect of the problem, and there may be others too. Thus, he is sufficiently cautious and alert. In case study, he studies each unit in its complete dimensions. The researcher, therefore, beings to feel as if he knows everything about the unit and needs no further enlightenment about it. It is quite comparable to our feeling of certainty about our neighbours or close friends whom we have lived for years together. Naturally we begin to feel that we know everything about them, but in reality a major part of their life is hidden from us. Even two brothers who have lived together for long years cannot understand the experiences and influences that have shaped their life. It is thus clear that case study, with all its defects and shortcomings, develops a false sense of confidence which is highly detrimental to any scientific outlook.
2. Generalisations are drawn from too few cases. Thus, what the researcher thinks to be the common trait of human nature may be personal peculiarity of the subject and therefore, applicable to particular person under particular circumstances.
3. The method is quite loose and unsystematic. No controls are exercised upon the informant or the researcher. The data collected in this way is generally incapable of verification and the generalisations drawn from it are also not very accurate.
4. There is enough scope for errors due to inaccurate observation and faulty inference, selection of a case that is not typical of the group, errors in the reporting,

failures of the memory, unconscious omission or repression of unpleasant facts, a tendency to dramatise facts, and describe what is more imaginary than real. Under such conditions the data collected and the inferences drawn are at times far from being valid.

5. The researcher develops a tendency towards *ad hoc* theorising. In place of finding some scientific explanation to a particular phenomena, he tries to find some commonsense explanation for it. He is so overconfident due to his intimate knowledge of the unit, that he begins to presume that even his commonsense or intuitive explanations, are most scientific. Such explanations, being incapable of verification, are hardly reliable.
6. The time and money needed for case study is much greater than in other methods. Even if 100 cases are studied under this method, it may very well take nearly two years. It may not only entail large financial expenditure, but there is also the problem of most of cases getting stray.
7. Read Bain has listed the following drawbacks of life history documents used in case study method:
   - (a) It does not provide impersonal, universal, non-ethical, non-practical, repetitive aspect of phenomena.
   - (b) The student may write what he thinks and what the investigator wants. The greater the rapport, the more subjective the whole process is.
   - (c) The subject is more likely to be self-justificatory than factual.
   - (d) The literary touch results in romantic over and understatement, convenient forgetting, and inclusion of many things that never happened.
   - (e) Case situations are seldom comparable. The subject tells his own story in his own words.

Problems of the Case Study Technique

Most of the difficulties in the use of this method can be reduced to one, although a more complex classification is possible. Interestingly enough, the basic danger in its use is the *response of the researcher*. The researcher comes to feel a false sense of certainty about his own conclusion. The danger, then, does not lie in any technical weakness of this approach or social processes or individuals as a whole.

The student may feel that this a constant danger in all research. Yet it should be remembered that in most research, there are constant remainders that a very narrow range of experience is represented by the data. However, long our interviews, gaps are all too obvious, and there is no way to fill them. However, each *case* which is developed as a unit takes on complete dimensions in the mind of the researcher. He comes to feel certain that he could answer many more questions about his case than can be answered from his file records. The case has a definite form and pattern, and as the researcher probes more deeply into the process or person being studied, he finds there are few surprises left. It is quite comparable to our feeling of certainty about our close friends, or the neighbourhood in which we have lived for years, or our families. There is, in short, an emotional feeling of certainty which is much stronger than in the case of other types of research. This is particularly true as compared with much survey work, in which the analyst has only the completed schedules before him and knows he cannot capture the varied experiences of the many interviewers who carried out those interviews.

Yet, the student can test the accuracy of his knowledge very easily, by submitting to questioning about his close friends or his own family, the "cases" he knows best. Most of us find that our feelings of certainty deceive us. We know far fewer data about these cases than we believe. Important facts are forgotten. Other facts are distorted, or surprising facets of these lives are unknown to us. For example, children usually believe that they "understand" their parents, but are often oblivious of many deep conflicts between them. Brothers and sisters are often unaware of important experiences happening to each other outside the family circle. What most of us feel is a kind of at-homeness with these close acquaintances, so that we fill in or ignore those facts or dimensions of the person which are really unknown to us.

This danger, then, is one which the observer *himself creates.* The *consequences* of this feeling of certainty are many, but most of them can be grouped under one main heading; *a temptation to ignore basic principles of research design.* Since the researcher is certain about the area of field he is investigating, he feels no need to check the overall design. For example, after the student has collected, say, 200 cases of juvenile delinquency from social-work records, supplemented by interviewing and other sources, it is difficult for him to feel that he does not have an adequate sample. The range of delinquency experience in his cases is so wide, the types of people so varied, the depth of detail so vivid, that the researcher ordinarily has a strong conviction that his selection is "representative". He was not, usually, following any known pattern of sampling, so that he feels certain there is no bias. It must be repeated at this point that we are not separating one type of researcher from any other type. *Any* investigator who absorbs the facts from a large number of cases will begin to feel that he really has a satisfactory sample, no matter how much knowledge he has about sampling design.

The result is, naturally, a strong temptation to extrapolate unwarrantedly. Perhaps, an equally important consequence of this feeling is the failure to make explicit just what are the generalisations underlying the analysis of the cases. One boy's refusal to give up his pilfering may be explained by his desire for economic gain. Yet, in a similar case, and without explaining the *bases* for the different explanation, another boy's refusal to give up thievery may be explained by his desire to humble his parents, a psycho-dynamic explanation. Although both explanations may be correct, we are likely to forget that any such analysis requires a *system* of explanation. It is not scientific to apply various explanations which by common sense or intuition seem to fit particular cases, on a purely *ad hoc* basis. Some set of generalisations is being used, and it is necessary to make explicit just why one or the other may or may not be applied. However, when the investigator feels so much "at home" with each case, he may be tempted to "feel" the right explanation—even though a second reader of our cases might come to an entirely different explanation. This is what is known as *ad hoc* theorising. The previous reference suggests a further danger resulting from this feeling of certainty; *the failure to test the reliability* of the data recorded, the classifications used, or the analysis of the data, as the researcher is likely to point out, no one else knows the data nearly so well as he, so that no one else could check his work adequately. Furthermore, case gathering is a time consuming activity, and it is difficult to find others who are willing to study the cases with such completeness.

Avoiding these problems: Nevertheless, these difficulties can be avoided by the student who is willing to follow good research planning. Being warned of the dangers which result from such a feeling of certainty, he will develop a research design which takes account of these dangers. He cannot avoid the feeling of certainty, but he can use an adequate sampling pattern. Knowing that his sampling is good, he has a rational basis for making estimates about the universe from which it was drawn. Instead of relying on intuition for his conclusions, he will make certain that whenever he analyzes a given factor, there are actual data for all case records concerning that factor. Further, he will develop his theoretical framework from the beginning of the research, so that he avoids speculations made on the spot to fit the peculiarities of each case.

Furthermore, he will attempt, as far as possible, to utilise the technique of qualitative coding for individual factors and traits which are amenable to such classifications. If he is to use categories like "selfish", or "adjusted", or "anomic", he will develop a set of instructions for deciding whether a given case falls into the category. If other investigators cannot use such instructions, they are likely to contain many implicit judgements, intuitions, common sense guesses, and the like. The good student will recognize that a description of research operations must be so written that other scientists can repeat them. If not, either the description or the operations are unclear. The student *must* make this test, if he is not to remain open to the charge from others that they "simply can't see" what he sees. It is usually good procedure to carry out this stage of analysis with the aid of a number of collaborators or assistants who can act as judges of the reliability of even simple classifications.

One may almost claim that it is at this point—that of developing categories, of defining and delimiting types of behaviour already recorded—that the case study requires the closest criticism. For it is at this stage that the systematisation of much of the mass of data begins, that is, condensation, excision, reinterpretation, etc. The final report cannot simply repeat the recorded observations. The steps in this transformation, then, must be carefully marked, if the researcher expects to have his conclusions accepted.

It is worth recording that this problem is not peculiar to sociology. When the historian begins to reduce the mass of individual observations from original sources, he faces the problem of showing his operations to fellow historians, so that they can follow them exactly, should they wish to do so. Much of the objection of social scientists to the published analyses of psychiatrists and psychoanalysts is simply that, whatever the details of the case, there is no clearly outlined set of operations by which the next scientist can use the same data to come to the same conclusion. The economist who studies the marketing process among tobacco farmers may find similarly that each case is so very different that colleagues are suspicious of conclusion until the operations of the analysis are made clear. As noted above, the best way of clarifying these steps is to develop definite coding instructions for most of the important qualitative items with definite tests for coding reliability.

IMPROVEMENT OF CASE STUDY METHOD

The various criticisms levelled against the use of case study method have not discouraged the social scientists to drop the method as unscientific, unsystematic and unfit for valid generalisation. On the other hand, they have made a determined effort to put the method on scientific lines. The names of Carl Rogers, Elton Mayo, Mirra Komarovsky, Alfred Kinsey and John Dollard require a particular mention in this respect. These social scientists have tried the improved techniques of collecting, recording and processing the case data.

Attempts have been made to quantify the case data and, thus, render it capable of statistical analysis, various kinds of socio-metric scales need a special mention in this respect. The use of schedules, structured interviews, uniform recording and various kinds of controls has been made, to arrive at a more scientific collection of data and valid generalisation from it.

John Dollard has set up the following standards for an adequate life history technique:

1. The subject must be viewed as a specimen in a cultural series.
2. The organic motors of action ascribed should be socially relevant.
3. The peculiar role of family group in transmitting the culture must be recognized.
4. The specific method of elaboration of organic materials into social behaviour must be shown.
5. The continuous related character of experience from childhood through adulthood must be stressed.
6. The social situation must be carefully and continuously specified as a factor.
7. The life history material must itself be organised and conceptualised.

In order to make the case data amenable to statistical treatment, an attempt is made to reduce the number of variables involved. Typological classification has been developed for this purpose. Such a classification can be mathematically treated by multiple factor analysis method as developed by Thurstone, Hotelling and Kelly, etc.

Making Case Study Effective

Above all, the utility of the case method largely depends on the ability and integrity of the investigator, if he really wants to take the pains of collecting the data in all possible systematic means. The study may be reliable. On the contrary, 'if the investigator is hasty and lacks wisdom in approach and fails to use appropriate methods of data collection, such cases only remain as cases and conclusion becomes meaningless. As indicated earlier case studies are the best method to derive what the investigator wanted. The observations of Alfred Marshall are highly relevant in revealing the true nature of case study method. About case study he commented as follows in his book *Principles of Economics:*

> "To work it (the case method) well, requires a rare combination of judgement in selecting cases, and of insight and sympathy in interpreting them. At its best, it is the best of all but in ordinary hands it is likely to suggest more untrustworthy general conclusions than those obtained by the extensive method of collecting more rapidly very numerous observations, reducing them as far as possible to statistical form and obtaining broad averages in which inaccuracies and idiosyncrasies may be twisted to counteract another to some extent."

Having considered the potentialities of the case method Carl Rogers, Alfred Kinsey, John Dollard and Elton Mayo have suggested some improvement in this method. The following points, deserve special mention here:

(i) The subject of study must be regarded as a specimen in a series of similar problems.

(ii) The life history material should be organised and properly conceptualised.

(iii) The technique of elaboration of organic materials into social behaviour must be properly specified.

(iv) The method of action should be socially relevant.

(v) The important role of any group or institution, which is responsible for transmitting a culture should be recognised.

(vi) In a case study relating to individuals, the continuously related experience from childhood should be stressed.

(vii) The social situation should be specified as part and parcel of the study.

It is in this context, Goode and Hatt emphasise on good research planning. Being warned off the dangers which result from such a feeling of certainty, the researcher will develop a research design which takes into account the difficulties. Perhaps, the researcher cannot avoid the feeling of certainty; but he can use an adequate sampling pattern. Knowing that his sampling is good, he has a rational basis for making estimates about the universe from which it was drawn. Instead of relying on intuition for his conclusions, he will make certain that whenever he analyses a given factor, there are actual data for all case records concerning that factor. Further, he will develop his theoretical framework from the beginning of the research so that he avoids speculation made on the spot to fit the peculiarities of each case.

Procedure for a Case Study

The case study has a systematic procedure involving the following important steps:

Define the problem

Each case has a problem or number of problems. A problem is the gap between what is desired and what is being achieved. The problem can be identified by reading the case. At the first reading, it is better to jot down the parts that you think are important. Then you might try to determine what the major or minor problems are jottings down, and how you might analyse them. In fact, in the first reading, whole of the problems may not be identified. Therefore, read the case again and find out through your preliminary analysis whether the impressions gathered by you in first reading are correct. At this stage, it may be possible to identify the nature or the subject-manager, worker, or organisation, as the case may be, its method of working, and how and why the problem has arisen.

Choice of cases

The first step in the case study is choosing the cases for indepth study. The researcher has to decide as to which unit has to be taken up for study. The unit of study may be an individual, or a group of persons or an institution or a group of institutions.

Collection of data

The collection of the data about the unit of study is the second step in the case study. The researcher may use different techniques and tools to collect data about the different aspects of the unit.

Analysis of data

The collected data has to be analysed. This is the third step. All the collected data are interrelated and analysed. The most dominant, the less dominant and neutral elements have to be observed. The relevant statistical techniques are to be used wherever necessary.

Identify the Alternatives

The problem around which the case is organised is amenable to solution by several possible alternatives. Some of which are obvious from the data of the case and from the definition of the problem. The alternatives which are not so obvious may be generated by the participants. At this stage, it is preferable to generate as many alternative as possible without evaluating the worth of each. This will provide opportunity to solve the problem at a much wider canvas.

Analyse the Alternatives

An analysis of alternatives comprises the break up of alternatives into parts with a view to (i) detecting the nature, proportion, and function of the parts and (ii) detecting the underlying relationships among a set of variables.

Interpreting and Reporting of Data

This is the final step in the procedure of a case study. After classification and analysis, the facts are explained, interpreted and then reported. The interpretation must be logical and coherent. The interpreted data must be finally brought out in a report form.

Variations of Case Study

Three major variations are found in the case study. They are: single case study, deviant case study and comparative or multiple case study.

Case Study Methods

We promote better management, a behavioural process, by training. Training is mainly to acquire those managerial skills which are short in a manager. Of all the methods adopted in learning/teaching techniques, the CASE STUDY method developed in 1910 in USA and now being propagated during the last decade or so, provides opportunities to both the teacher and the taught to promote managerial understanding and competence, since it helps in contemplation and discussion of the actual situation. It is a wrong notion that the case studies are confined to management students. Cases may pertain to any discipline, from sociology to sexology and from psychology to astrology where skills for solving complex unstructured problems or preparing plans are required. The origin of the case study methods itself is from Harvard Lawyers. Cases may describe problems facing individuals, groups, institutions or even nations.

Cases are different from 'exercises'. An exercise is to learn and apply a particular concept, technique or principle. A case is to learn a broad range of skills and has many alternatives, while an exercise has only one situation and one way of reaching that solution. Case studies are to practice and attain analytical and communicative skills.

A case, as defined by Reynolds, is a short description in words and numbers, of an actual management situation. It describes the present and past position of the situation and the problem that is posed. All the data are provided. A case consisting the history of the situation may be small or lengthy. Small ones may be lacking particulars and hence may be taxing with more assumptions than realities, while lengthy ones may not project the conflict correctly and therefore, solution may seem easy without much alternatives. All available information may not be sufficient and at the time of analysing a case, further information may have to be injected.

A written case study could be anything from 300 to 6000 words long. The length will depend on the purpose for which it is being used, type of participants and availability of time. The parts of a case study generally are:

1. A Subject (Example: Customer relations)
2. A Setting (Example: The office of Manager—Marketing)
3. Data (Example: Nature and number of complaints—received by the department.
4. Background (Example: Type of complaints from customers, dealers, officials, others, etc.)

Once the above particulars have been decided, further writing only consists of description, characterisation and narration. These elements could directly be combined and written into the case study or first thought out and written separately and then put together. The description should not be too long. The description should be in a simple easy to understand language. There should not be too many characters and each should be carefully thought of in terms of personality traits. The term 'narration' refers to the plot or sequence of events which may be developed upto a climax and then participants asked to think about what follows or possible solutions to the problems.

The habit of logical thinking and conceptualisation can be developed through a systematic study of cases. Analysis of cases enables arguing viewpoints with peers and this again develops good communicative skills. A case study can be stated to be the midway between a real world project and an exercise.

Thus, a case study method of learning helps in developing skills on alternatives and decision-making. Case studies simulate environment. Case studies are to help 'creative' problem-solving techniques. According to Geofftaston (*Learning from Case Studies* 1982. Prentice Hall, 1982) the following six **major skill areas** are developed through case studies.

1. Analytical skills

One learns to classify, organise, and evaluate the information handled. Using this information, one attempts to understand the situation as described, this is, however, fraught with the danger of not thinking logically when the information is taxing.

2. Application skills

This is at a lower level where concepts and principles are applied e.g., discounted cash flow.

3. Creative skills

Unlike an exercise which may be solved by logical process also, cases cannot be solved by logical process alone. Creativity is a vital quality for a manager and is more useful in decision-making.

4. Communicative skills

By writing well construed reports, analysis and by discussions, both written and oral communicative skills are developed.

5. Social skills

Case discussions are essentially social processes. One learns to communicate, listen, support, argue, control oneself, etc. In fact, there is a belief that case courses are more of human behaviour than problem-solving.

6. Self-analysis skills

A case is always useful in application of the situation to oneself and analyse the situation with reference to self. Thus, it helps in self-improvement.

Benefits of the case study are that through the group discussion, a participant can form a more objective view or/and express reasonably in the presence of others. It helps in improving the skills of logical deduction and analysis. The methods, are therefore, often best suited to attitude development.

There are several management problems where there are no clear cut solutions. While dealing with such issues one of the best tools available is the case study. One can draw upon a wealth of experience by the case study method since the cases themselves are generally developed from experience.

The case study can serve several **purposes**. Some of them are:

1. It can be used as a cautionary story so that the participants do not repeat the mistakes committed by others (e.g., concept of many safety errors).

2. May be used for arriving at general conclusions on important management principles from specific samples (e.g., concept of delegation).
3. Practicing techniques are applying principles in the risk free environment of a classroom (e.g., making an investment decision based on supplied information).
4. Extending experience by role-playing various parts which often cannot be done in real life (e.g., be able to view a problem from someone else's point of view say, through the eyes of a Finance Manager).

In a developing country like India, there are certain limitations and constraints in using the case study method, although this is an innovative technique in improving managerial skills. There are various problems like lingua franca, socio-political and cultural milieu, religious fervours, shyness of the participants, secrecy in sharing of information, lack of professional skills and non-acceptance of existence of such skills. Problems in dissemination of information and dissipation of details are the other constraints. Impatience of participants in going through lengthy case studies replete with details and criticism about short cases deplete with information and lack of depth of knowledge or time constraints are other problems.

There is no emphatic right or wrong solution or recommendations for any case study. The problem can be solved in many ways and in a given situation, only a few of the visible alternatives would be relevant or feasible. In spite of all the constraints, case study method is an extremely important tool in imparting managerial skills, creativity and creative skills are most essential for managers. Case studies create thinking power and analytical skills more essentially required at all levels.

This book contains thirty-one case studies mostly suited to Indian situations. These cases will serve as model. These case studies are from real life-like situations.

PART B

CASE STUDY—A GUIDE TO ANALYSIS

Case Study—A Guide to Analysis

HOW TO STUDY A CASE?

Introduction

Case method requires students to do most of their studying before class, as contrasted with the lecture method in which most of the study occurs after the class notes are reviewed. If you want to understand fully the arguments and presentation of your fellow students in this class, apart from your own presentation, you must be prepared beforehand.

A typical case consists of pages of prose description. It often includes some quantitative prose or presentations in the form of charts, graphs, tables, monograph, organisation charts, factory layout, etc. Cases may include any type of material that can be printed.

1. Steps in case study

Read the case thorough once very quickly. The purpose of this reading is to make you familiar with the topic, the characters, the general nature and quality of the evidence with which you must work and some idea of the problems that must be noted.

Read the case thoroughly a second time, at a much slower and more thoughtful rate. Take note of important facts in this prose passage and study each quantitative exhibit. By this, you should be able to abstract from this case, a statement of the problems involved, the nature of the decisions facing the manager and most of the margin elements such as constraints, opportunities and strengths and resources which influence the action of the manager.

Finally recheck the various important facts you have previously identified to make sure that your view of the solution is consistent with all the facts.

2. A general problem-solving format

The various elements of problem-solving are:

(a) identifying the problem(s) or areas of improvement;

(b) setting objectives for achievement;

(c) identifying possible alternative course of action;

(d) predicting the likely consequences of each course of action;

(e) choosing and implementing the course action whose expected outcome most nearly matches the desired outcome or objectives.

3. Steps in problem-solving

(a) Analyse the present situation.

(b) Forecast the future situation.

(c) Set objectives.

(d) Define problems.

(e) List possible alternative courses of action.

(f) Predict the outcomes of alternative courses of action.

(g) Compare, choose and implement the best course of action.

4. How to participate in a case discussion

Each student prepares the case analysis without any pre-class discussion with other students. The class consists of presentatives of one student viewpoint after another. Depending upon the teacher's preferences, students may be asked to make fairly detailed complete statements of their arguments or they may be encouraged to offer shorter statements selected from their analysis at appropriate points with development of the class discussion. The eventual outcomes of class discussion of individual efforts will usually be the development of general agreement about the relative merits of small number of possible courses of action.

5. How to write a case analysis paper

The body of the report should follow the following order:

(a) Important facts about the present situation.

(b) Forecast of changes in the situations.

(c) Objectives for the future and the problems which arise because the current situation fails short of future goals.

(d) Alternative actions that must be taken with predicted consequences of each alternative.

(e) Description in detail of the recommended action and its implementation.

Questions for Case Study Analysis

1. What is going on here?
2. Is there a problem at all?
3. What precisely is the problem?
4. What has caused it?
5. Are we looking at cases or symptoms?
6. What are the main issues?
7. Why are these issues important?
8. Whose problem is it?
9. What precisely are the objectives?
10. What should he try to do now?
11. What possible courses of actions are open?
12. How realistic is each of the actions/solutions proposed?
13. What are their possible effects?

PREPARING A CASE

A case may be prepared for:

1. Oral analysis for discussion (by individuals)
2. Oral analysis for discussion (by groups)
3. Written analysis (by individuals)
4. Written analysis (by groups)
5. Oral/written analysis and presentation (by individuals/ groups)

What particular method would be followed in the counselling sessions would depend upon the thinking of the counsellor and other factors, including the nature of the company and the length of the case. For many students, this will be their first real exposure to case analysis. For facilitating your analysis, we have given or posed some questions at the end of each case. You may analyse the case along these questions and in the process follow the line of action, as stated below:

A Guide for Case Preparation

Environmental Analysis: *(Threats and opportunities)*

1. Identify Strategic issues.
2. Describe past and present strategies.
3. Evaluate past and present strategies in terms of organisation mission.
4. Determine strategies you will recommend.
5. Show how your strategies improve mission accomplishment.

The counsellor may ask one of the students who has prepared the case to make a presentation on one of the questions. This can then be followed by an open discussion. After all the questions have been covered one by one, the case as a whole can then be thrown open for discussion. The counsellor towards the end can sum up the whole analysis and draw some conclusions. Whether the counsellor asks for oral discussion or written presentation, it is always advisable to prepare a written analysis. Apart from several other benefits, it will bring to the case a thoroughness which is generally not expected when you prepare for oral discussion.

While no standard procedure can be laid down, the following successive steps will be helpful for analysing the case (whether for oral discussion or written presentation):

1. know the facts;
2. understand the environment of the organisation (external and internal);
3. gather relevant information from outside sources, if necessary;

4. appraise and evaluate the environment;
5. consider and keep in mind the mission of the organisation, while making recommendations.

A case is a technical paper. As such it deserves careful reading. A good approach is to read the case three times; once rapidly, scanning quickly any exhibits; a second time thoroughly and slowly, putting careful attention to the exhibits and making some notes about apparent organisational objectives, strategies, symptoms of problems, root causes, unresolved issues and the role of key individuals; and a third time rapidly again to reinforce the main points.

While analysing the case, try to look for issues beneath the surface. For instance, at first glance, the issue might appear to be whether or not there is ample demand for the product at the current selling price. On closer examination, you might find that it is the method of compensating or providing incentives to the sales force that is standing in the way of achieving higher sales volume.

To help diagnose the situation, put yourself in the position of the manager or managerial group portrayed in the case and get attuned to the overall environment facing the management. You may expect the case to contain several problems and issues rather than just one.

Sometimes a case may not contain all the information that you think is necessary for analysing the case. This may be particularly true with regard to data on external environment, competitors and industry characteristics. This often requires library research using business magazines, trade journals, company Annual Report, etc. While searching for information, it should be borne in mind that all facts are not equally important. A systematic approach to information gathering should be followed.

While analysing and recommending any course of action, you may always keep in mind the mission of the organisation. Ultimately, all aspects of strategic management must be related with the mission of the organisation. For ascertaining the mission of the organisation, you may attempt to answer this question: What is the organisation trying to do and for whom? In examining the mission of the organisation, you may consider from both descriptive and normative standpoints. Where necessary, you may not shy away from taking a normative view and evaluating management from an ethical or moral standpoint.

The arguments you make and the positions you take should be defensible and supportable with evidence (statistical data, calculations, etc.). Your objective should be to develop what you think is a pragmatic, advisable course of action that is based on a serious analysis of the situation. Someone else might have evaluated the same facts in another way and thus has a different "right" solution. While defending your own answer, you should also try to relate it with the answers of other participants and try to appreciate the reasons behind any difference. Though the case method is a group process, it does not imply conformity to group opinion. Sometimes one has to swim against the tide of majority opinion. In the practice of management, there is always room for originality and unorthodoxy.

While discussing or arguing your point, you can assume that the other participants know the facts or what "the case says". Therefore, rehashing the information should be held to the minimum except when you need to document, compare or support your position. Be as specific as possible in your comments and provide comparative data. Take for instance the slight growth in market share from 10 per cent in 1993 to 11 per cent in 1999 was achieved during a general recession and in an industry growing at about 8 per cent annually. While analysing, recognise the distinction between facts and opinions given in the case.

Once you have thoroughly diagnosed the company's situation and weighed the pros and cons of various alternative courses of action, you may decide on what the company should do to tackle the problems or improve its performance. Draw up your set of recommendations and prepare an "action agenda". This is the most crucial part of the analysis. Bear in mind that proposing realistic, workable solution is not the same as offering a hasty, or not a properly conceived possibility. Do not recommend anything you would not be prepared to do yourself if you were in the shoes of the decision-maker.

SOURCE OF CASE DATA

Following are the main sources of case data:

1. Personal documents—diaries, autobiography, memories letters, etc.
2. Life history.

1. Personal Documents

Most of the people keep diaries, write their autobiographies, memoir or memories. These personal documents contain the description of the remarkable events of the life narrator as well as his reactions towards them. They may also contain the description of even those events in which he has played his part only a witness of a distant spectator. According to Allport they are self-revealing records which intentionally or unintentionally yield direct information regarding the structure, dynamics and functioning of author's mental life. Such personal documents, although sufficiently subjective in nature are highly important for social research. Diaries are mostly written for self-satisfaction and the writer is not likely to distort facts deliberately. Such documents may be written for general purpose and later on used by the researcher, or they may be specially kept for the purpose of research. The former type is generally more reliable, although it may fail to give full facts.

According to Pauline Young, "Personal documents represent continuity experience which helps to illuminate the writer's personality, social relations and philosophy of life often expressed in objective reality or subjective appreciation." They are, thus, very helpful in studying the personality of the writer and his reactions to different circumstances of life. As the writer is an identical part of the group, they may represent not only the reactions of the person but of any typical member of the group.

2. Life History

Life history is the study of various events of respondent's life together with an attempt to find their social significance. It is in this way that life history differs from the pure historical narrative of facts. While the pure narrative aims at narrating the facts only, life history aims at revealing the meaning and significance of these events in the context of motivating factors of social life. It is, thus, a combination of facts and the inferences. Life history data is generally gathered through prolonged interviews with the respondents, use of any written material available about his life and the analysis of the facts so collected in order to draw valid generalisations from them.

Case studies, thus, generally take to form the use of written material about the respondent and the collection of data through interviews. Besides this, various other methods may be adopted to gather the correct information. According to Mrs Young, they may include from simple verification method *viz.*, periodical conferences, impromptu conversations, dramatic productions, observation and post-experimental interviews, to more complicated processes like experimental studies, a wide range of tests including hypnotic tests, tests of ability, tests of aesthetic appreciation, emotional conditioning, social reaction to frustration, imaginal productivity, psychological insight, etc. The entire range of informant's life from childhood to old age is thoroughly enquired and tested and every aspect of life is taken into consideration.

Some Sources of Case Material in India

1. **Institutional sources:** There are institutions such as Indian Institute of Management, Ahmedabad and Administrative Staff College of India, Hyderabad that provide case material.
2. **Periodicals:** Magazines such as Business India, Business World, etc. provide several types of interesting industry and corporate reports. Though these reports are not written for the purpose of case analysis, they can be adapted suitably for use in case discussion. News papers such as *The Economic Times*, *Financial Express*,

The Hindu, etc. give extensive coverage and special supplements on industries and companies which can be used for analysis.

3. **Books:** There is a dearth of books providing case in Business Policy. Most recent publications in Business Policy, however, include case studies that can be used for class discussion. Here are some books that exclusively provide cases:
   (a) *Problems in Management*, ASCI Case Collection, First (1962) and Second (1967) series (Mumbai: Asia Publishing House).
   (b) S.S. Khera, *Cases in Indian Administration* (New Delhi: Indian Institute of Public Administration, 1963).
   (c) Franscis A. Menezes, *Cases in Management* (New Delhi: Tata McGraw-Hill).
   (d) BS K.S. Chopra, *Cases in Corporate Planning* (Pune: The Times Research Foundation, 1989).

Guidelines to Make a Good Presentation of Case

1. Read the case once for familiarity so that you get a 'feel' of the situation described in the case.
2. Read the case again for grasping the facts. Make notes and jot down important points.
3. Evaluate the situation described in the case. Attempt to gain an understanding of the objectives, strategies, policies, problems, causes of problems, issues, and the roles of key individuals.
4. Prepare the environmental threats and opportunities profile (ETOP) and strategic advantages profile (SAP).
5. Think of strategic alternatives and suggest the 'best' option and support your proposal with facts, reasons, and arguments.
6. Propose a comprehensive plan for strategy implementation. Keep in mind the feasibility of implementing your suggested strategy, considering the

availability of resources, and whether or not the strategic changes will be manageable.

7. Evaluate your proposal; state the quantitative and qualitative criteria for evaluating strategy and state the assumptions you have made in arriving at conclusions. Suggest contingency plans.
8. Prepare notes for oral and written presentation or for participating in group discussions.

The guidelines given above are not meant to be rigidly followed. Rather, each case would call for a unique approach. Not all cases require a comprehensive analysis as suggested above. Some cases are short and need specific analysis pertaining to only one or two aspects of strategic management. But it is good to know the right approach to follow, specially if one is attempting a case analysis for the first time.

Written Presentation

We had earlier suggested that even when your counsellor has asked you to prepare your analysis for oral discussion in the class, it is advisable to analyse the case in writing. Your counsellor sometimes may specifically ask you to do a written analysis so that he could evaluate your analysis and provide you with some useful feedback. A written presentation is a more structured approach to case analysis. Just as there is no set formula for preparing a case for oral discussion, so there is no set procedure for a written case analysis either. If questions are given, in the case, you may attempt your analysis based on those questions. In case no questions are given, you may attempt a comprehensive written analysis (without being unduly lengthy) on the lines suggested.

In written presentation you should avoid repetition, exaggeration and over-generalisation. If your analysis involves some important quantitative calculations, then you should use tables and charts to present the data clearly and efficiently. You can also use flow-charts and diagrams wherever appropriate. Use sub-headings to organise your report and put all your analysis in a logical sequence. It is not advisable to just tack the exhibits at the end of your report and let the reader figure out what they mean and why they have been included. Instead, cite some of the key numbers and summarise the conclusions (to be drawn from the exhibits) in the body of the text itself and refer the reader to the charts and exhibits for more detail. It goes without saying that your report should be properly organised and written in a communicative and persuasive manner.

While stating your recommendations, see that they are in sufficient detail so as to be meaningful. Simply making a statement like "the firm should improve its market position", or "the organisation should do more planning" is not enough. You must explain what you think must be done. You must say how your plan should be implemented. In other words, offer a definite agenda for action, stipulate a time-table and sequence for initiating actions, indicating and suggesting who should be responsible for doing what.

Frequently, participants in the case method are required to make written analysis of cases. In doing so, it is important to keep in mind the guidelines that we suggested for preparation for case discussion. Written assignments are now a part of continuous evaluation in management courses. Examination papers in Business Policy usually include a case for analysis.

We suggest that you should take additional care in making the written analysis of a case:

1. Keep the written analysis simple but do not overlook major issues.
2. Adopt a nice style of writing, use headings, labels, and topic sentences, and put the whole structure in an integrated and logical manner.
3. Include analysis based on techniques wherever relevant. ETOP, SAP, ratio analysis, portfolio analysis, etc. are some of the techniques that can be used with good results.
4. Specifically state the assumptions when making recommendations, provide supporting evidence, and benchmarks for evaluation.
5. Provide a summary, in a page, of the major issues and recommendations made by you.

Oral Presentation

With regard to oral presentation of cases, some points have to be kept in mind. We suggest some guidelines that can help you to make a good oral presentation:

1. Plan well in advance because oral presentation is a difficult—but rewarding experience.
2. Do not commit the mistake of reading out a written analysis of case. Oral presentation has to be even more precise and convincing. There is not much time available for making lengthy analysis and arguments.
3. Use teaching aids such as blackboard, overhead projector, etc. to present charts and diagrams for enhancing the value of your presentation. Remember: "A picture is worth a thousand words."
4. Rehearse your presentation and be prepared to handle questions from the instructor and fellow participants.

In making an oral presentation, usually the role assumed by a participant is that of a third neutral party or a consultant. In this way, it is possible to make a detached and thorough analysis. Sometimes, the method adopted for oral presentation may be that of role playing. This method is similar to the presentation of a play or a drama. Participants may assume the roles described in the case and then actually play the roles before an audience. But it is worthwhile to remember that role playing is a serious exercise and is not to be used as an opportunity to display theatrical skills.

Group Discussion

Several management institutions in India admit students by a selection process that has group discussion as one of the elements. Selection and recruitment of management trainees and middle-level managers by companies also may be based on group discussion. This form of case analysis, therefore, has much to offer to students. Group discussion for strategic management case analysis offers an excellent opportunity to participants to develop communication skills. Also, group discussion is a more realistic process as most strategic decisions are actually made by managers in a group setting.

Here are a few guidelines to enable you to make a better analysis and participate effectively in group discussions:

1. Preparing the case thoroughly by all participants is an essential prerequisite for effective discussion. So, make sure that you have all the facts before participating in a group discussion.
2. A preliminary small group discussion could be informally had before the actual discussion takes place.
3. Group discussion involves challenging someone else's position or defending one's own. This has to be done on the basis of facts, figures, reason, and not by being aggressive method.
4. Keep the principles of effective intergroup behaviour in mind: be communicative and participative; expect and tolerate dissenting views; contribute rather than just talk; and learn to work as a team.
5. Observe that your fellow participants, put forth several ideas that probably did not occur to you. Group discussion offers a chance to realise that it is not good to adopt a rigid stand (a firm stand is, of course, different from a rigid stand). Do not be afraid to express your views but at the same time realise that ultimately group performance is tied to the performance of individual members.

With these guidelines in mind, it is possible for you to make good use of the group discussion approach to case analysis.

We have provided some simple guidelines and ideas for effective preparation for case discussion, doing written analysis of cases, and presenting analysis orally and in a group. At the end of this note on the case method, you will find a select bibliography that provides major source books for further reading.

Industry Analysis

Case analysis is done for organisations, while industry analysis is of a whole industry. Industry analysis is done on the basis of industry profile which is actually a case of the industry. The usual contents of an industry profile are: history of the industry, stage of life cycle, major companies, buyer-side and demand-side patterns and conditions, state of competition, capital requirements, technology level, role and impact of government policies, skill and resources availability and future prospects.

The purpose of industry analysis is three-fold:

1. To identify strategic issues and problems facing the industry.
2. To identify the strengths, weakness, opportunities, threats, key success factors, and other strategically relevant aspects of an industry.
3. To evaluate a business's competitive position and future prospects.

In fact, while preparing case analysis, it is desirable to perform a preliminary industry analysis. This provides a good idea of what alternatives a company has; what prospects does each of the alternatives have; and what would be the best strategic alternative for a company. Industry analysis can also help in supporting strategic choice with a wider information base and greater in-depth understanding of industry and competitive factors.

Concluding Comments

The case method is a powerful pedagogical tool and benefits from using it, for learning strategic management, usually overflow to other areas as well. For instance, by analysis of cases, you will not only learn about companies but also get acquainted with the industry in which those companies exist, other companies with which a firm competes, the specific and general business environment for a number of firms and government policies and regulatory framework within which firms operate. At another level you get a good idea of how different individuals acted in a given situation, how others reacted and how important organisational processes like decision-making actually take place. Veritably, case analysis is a highly effective experiential exercise. The remaining part of this book contains 31 cases which can be used for analysis.

The theory, practice and cases in this book are all aimed at making you a better learner and practitioner of strategic management. We wish that you are successful in achieving this purpose.

What an Evaluator Looks for in a Case Analysis?

The important elements that a counsellor (or evaluator) would generally look for in a case analysis are:

1. Care with which focus and background knowledge have been used.
2. Ability to state problems and issues clearly.
3. Use of appropriate analytical techniques.
4. Evidence of sound logic and arguments.
5. Consistency between analysis and recommendations.
6. Ability to formulate reasonable and feasible recommendations for action.

Conclusion

Case preparation and presentation is challenging as well as rewarding. As you develop and refine your skills which are, perhaps, not as obvious as the knowledge gained in a lecture, you find that they apply to numerous situations in your professional and personal life. Remember that each case requires significant amount of time if you are really interested in making a good analysis. Without this, case analysis will not do much good to you.

Analytical Tools for Case Study

There are a number of tools which have been found to be useful both academically and professionally. Among the more important ones are:

1. SWOT Analysis
2. Ratio Analysis
3. Portolio Analysis
4. Checklist (Strategic audit)

CASE ANALYSIS
A HARVARD BUSINESS SCHOOL APPROACH, 1990

Prelude

This Methodology of Approaching a case comes from the '*Systems*' concept to Management and is commonly known as the 8-Plan Approach to Business cases. However, the steps involved need not be construed as a strick watertight compartment for solving a particular case. The astonishing fact is that, both *Americans* and *Britishers* jointly acknowledge this to be an ideal approach. The Approach can be applied to all disciplines of management, with a careful study of the various factors to be eliminated and included during the course of analysis depending on the Area of Study. Mastery is achieved on your ability to sift one variable from the other, which largely comes out of your Broad-based view of the Business Milieu and the Empirical Skills gathered. While the case approach exhibits some amount of difficulty at the earlier stages, it will become a Handy, Easy and Practical Approach in solving cases at later periods. Let us start going through the stages with one famous quotation of Peter F. Drucker:

"There are Always Better Solution in Business."

The 8-Plan Approach

A given case can be analysed only to the extent of the data given in the case and influence from external variables on the company, to a certain extent has to be assumed. Hence, it is a worthwhile practice to start the analysis with a conditional clause as follows:

> "The analysis has been done to the extent of data available and influence from the external environment has been subjected to an empirical and conceptual understanding, apart from what is enunciated in the case."

Only the headings of various analysis areas are to be bold and underlined. All other factors have to be touched individually in paragraphs with the first word(s) alone in capitals to convey the message of the paragraph. An alternative way, may be to go in a points for us.

Step 1: Character role analysis

In this step, we are basically trying to figure out the various names (characters) and their role in the organisation.

(E.g.) Mr. X — Asst. Manager — Sales.
Mr. Y — Finance Manager.
Mr. Z — Vice President — Marketing.

In large cases, here are often, too many characters, where we lose time, recalling their roles. The above step can help you throughout the entire case. This step also makes the analyser comfortable in being able to establish his confidence over solving the case.

Step 2: Situational analysis

In this step, a Micro-Swot analysis is being done. Strengths and weakness refer to the Micro (or) the Internal Environment, while opportunities and threats refer to the Macro (or); External Environment. The situational Analysis, has to be done only to the extent of data available. If we are given a particular market of operation say EEC, Asia-Pacific, etc., then, we can probably analyse the influence of the external factors, as otherwise, it is a healthy trend to stop making assumptions about the external environment. This step essentially helps you in finding the exact situation of the company under study, so that your direction of priority gets shifted.

Accordingly, answering question like:

(a) Is it more of a Marketing/Financial/Production oriented?

(b) Is it the uncontrollable Macro Environment, Personnel Problem? that is playing a major part?

Step 3: Problem(s)—Function analysis

The earlier step helps you in finding roughly as to where the problem lies but not the exact problem(s) and their respective functional areas. In this step, we're going to list out the actual problems and the related functional areas. Whatever problem(s) you find in functional area, you can list them and at a later step, select only the actual problems.

(E.g.) SALES — Inefficient Training and Poor Product Knowledge.

PRODUCTION — Poor vendor rating and low quality of supplies.

Step 4: Sifting problems from causes

What may be perceived as problems in the earlier step have to be now separated as *Causative Factors* and *Problems*. If causes have been diagnosed as a problem, you may take the entire case on a Wrong Track. So use *Cause-Effect* Argument to each of the problems you have studied in the earlier step and try to separate the problems from causes and arrange each of the problems with the corresponding causes. The *Problems* you settle for at this step are going to be carried on till the end of the analysis process.

(E.g.) A low sales promotion budget may lead to very low investment on POP Materials which would have brought down counter sales. Here, don't claim the two former elements as problems, for they are only causes to the final problem of low counter sales.

Step 5: Cost analysis

In this step, you are going to analyse the Real (or) opportunity cost of the various problems, enlisted in the last step. If as in the above example, the Real cost of low counter sales has resulted in a deficit of Rs. 2 crore from the set forecast, then that is described as the *Real Cost*. However, if the Problem is of wrong selection of a medium of advertisement, and a resultant decrease of Rs. 2 crore arises in sales, then that is categorised as the opportunity cost of non-utilisation of the right medium of advertisement. There are situations which you cannot assign a cost factor to a problem. In such cases, it is your individual judgement which counter.

Step 6: Analysis of identifiable central problem

If all the earlier steps have been done with due caution, this step can help you in figuring out the central problem in a clear way. Naturally, the central problem is one which has the major cost (Real opportunity). In the earlier step, if the cost could not be quantified, the repercussions or the effect of the problem (end-result) can be studied and its intensity found. Here, when you settle for a particular problem to be the central problem, take its set of causes, which may be taken from Step 4. This will help you in arriving at possible ways of remedying the situation (problem). The central problem arrived at should, to a major extent, be the root cause of other problems. Sometimes, a situation with 2 to 3 problems having the same cost may be experienced, in which case, they have to be taken together for solving.

Step 7: Avenues of rectification

We have a central problem. We are getting into the process of evolving various alternatives to reduce the cost of that problem(s). Here, the causes for the problem(s) will be of great help in developing alternatives to solve the problem.

Step 8: The optimum alternative(s) and impact

On the similar lines of selecting the central problem(s), by the cost factors attached to it, here, we are going to select the *Optimum Alternative(s)* on the basis of following factors:

(a) *Optimality* of the alternative towards solution
(b) *Time-consciousness*
(c) *Cost Effectiveness*
(d) *Feasibility*
(e) *Viability* (depending upon the problem possessing a commercial motive or not).

Next step: Try out an Actual case.

SELECT BIBLIOGRAPHY ON THE CASE METHOD

Andrews, K.R. (Ed.), *The Case Method of Teaching Human Relations and Administration* (Cambridge, Mass: Harvard University Press, 1953).

Bhardwaj, S., *Case Study Method—Theory and Practice* (New Delhi: National Books Organisation, 1989).

Note: This book is in the area of public administration and management.

Gokhale, S., *Cases in Personnel Management* (Pune, 1981).

I.L.O., *An Introductory Course in Teaching and Training for Management Development* (Geneva: International Labour Office, 1972).

McNair, M.P. and A.C. Hersum, *The Case Method at Harvard Business School* (New York, McGraw-Hill, 1954).

Ramaswami, T.R., *Indian Case Studies*, T.R. Publications, Madras.

Reynolds, J.I., *Case Method in Management: Development—Guide for Effective Use, Management Development Series* No. 17 of I.L.O. Geneva (New Delhi: Oxford & IBH Publishing, 1980).

PART C

CASE STUDY—HOW TO ARRIVE AT A SOLUTION—A PRACTICAL APPROACH

Case Study—How to Arrive at a Solution—A Practical Approach

CASE NO. 1
DILEMMA

'Arjuna Trading Company' is an engineering concern and has branches in as many as ten states and union territories of India.

The establishment has over 7000 employees including 1150 officers. The organisation though spread over in different cities, has a common seniority both for officers and workmen.

The organisation, very generously encourages sports and sportsmen and has a good number of teams participating in various local and State Tournaments. Arjuna Trading Company also has individual officers and workmen participating in different tournaments in individual games such as Tennis, Badminton, Table Tennis, Chess, etc.

One of the middle-level officers of the company achieved an extraordinary standard in Tennis and has won, in his individual capacity, first the State title, then the National title and then the International title. Arjuna Trading Co. was proud of this employee and gave him every facility to develop himself. In one year when the middle-level officer won a triple crown in All India Championships and also Championship in two international prestigious tournaments, the local Chief Manager under whom he was working, was immensely impressed by the performance.

The Chief Manager, thus, impressed by his performance in the sports field, promoted him straight five steps above his own level. Normally, for his colleagues in the same grade, it would take about fourteen years to reach the level and that too by appearing for different examinations and interviews (for judging suitability) conducted by the management.

It so happened that one of the workmen of the Arjuna Trading Co. had also obtained sufficient expertise and skill to represent the State in the basketball team. He has been the Captain of the Basketball team of the establishment. He also represented as a very dependable player in the basketball team at State level with definite potential of representing National level in due course. The trade union, operating in the establishment, while thanking and congratulating the management for promoting the officer, five ranks above his own, for the splendid performance in sports, also requested the management to show similar gesture for this workman who has reached a level of representing the State team. The union leader argued that in spite of the worker's poor circumstances and generally unfavourable conditions of life, his attaining the expertise to reach a standard of representing State level team, is, perhaps, as good as the officer's feat of attaining international standard. The trade union, therefore, expressed its hope that the management would promote the workman for his sports activities also five ranks above, as was done for the officer for his purely sports activity.

Questions

1. If you are the General Manager, how would you view the action of the Manager in promoting the officer five ranks above purely on his achievement in the field of Sports?
2. What would be your decision, in so far as, the request of the trade union for similar jumps to the workman concerned?
3. How would you argue and what would be your rationale if you do not want to grant five jumps to the worker? Since the workmen are governed by labour legislation, unlike the officers, can they seek legal remedy. If so, how would you tackle the matter?

4. Would you think of a directive/administrative order for future guidance of the managerial staff, if so, what would be the salient features of the directive?

Summary of the Case

Arjuna Trading Company is an engineering concern. It has branches all over India. There are 7000 employees including 1150 officers. The company has one common seniority list. The company encourages sportsmen and players. One middle level officer secured both national and international championship in sports. His local chief manager promoted him five steps above his own level, which he could reach only after 14 years that too after success in written and oral tests. Another low level worker is the captain of the state level basketball team. He was a poor worker with poor living conditions. The Trade Union requested management to promote this worker just like the previous middle level officer.

Problem No. 1 of the case:

1. Common seniority list is a defective policy.

Problem No. 2 of the case:

2. Lack of promotion norms.

Problem No. 3 of the case:

3. Defective approach towards the attainment in non-work performance.

First Alternative Answers to the Questions:

Ans. to Q. No. 1. The promotion given to the middle level officer for his attainment in sports is correct. There is nothing wrong in the action of the local chief manager in this matter.

Ans. to Q. No. 2. I would yield to the request of the Trade Union for such similar promotion to the low level worker who is the captain of the state level basketball team.

Ans. to Q. No. 3. The workers can seek legal remedy if they are not promoted for their achievements in sports and games through the court of law/legal remedy. The management in consultation with the Trade Union may formulate a new norm acceptable for both sides to avoid any further rift in the future, if the management wants.

Ans. to Q. No. 4. There is no need for a new directive/ administrative order.

Second Alternative Answers to the Questions:

Ans. to Q. No. 1. If I were the General Manager, I would not promote the employee purely for his achievements in sports.

Ans. to Q. No. 2. I would not yield to the request of the Trade Union for such similar promotion to the low level worker. Because he is not both technically and educationally qualified worker for 5 jumps in his career.

Ans. to Q. No. 3. In my opinion instead of giving promotion, it is better to offer appreciation/felicitation/one or two increments/ cash award, by the management. From the General Fund of the Trade Union, the worker may be paid some amount as a token of appreciation. Career promotion must be decided on the basis of the experience-cum-efficiency of the worker along with test and interview.

The workers cannot seek legal remedy if they are not promoted purely on the basis of their achievements in sports and games. The problem can be tackled by formulating cadre-wise seniority list and uniform norms for promotion in consultation with the Trade Union/Works Committee because Trade Union can convert an individual dispute into industrial dispute. Standing Order may be prescribed relating to these matters.

Ans. to Q. No. 4. There is a need for a directive/ administrative order for the future guidance of the managerial staff. The salient features of the directive should be following:

- (i) Employees must be broadly divided into three categories viz., top, middle and low level employees, with sub-divisions.
- (ii) For each category of workers separate seniority list must be prepared.
- (iii) Time bound promotion with weightage for work performance/efficiency must be introduced.
- (iv) Appraisal/evaluation must be introduced.

(v) Cash award/facilities and special concessions may be given for the achievements in sports, games and for appreciable public achievements. For example, more favourable rules than the Statutory Leave Rules relating to "Annual Leave with Wages" may be framed for such type of workers by the management.

CASE NO. 2
CHOICE OF A LEADER

Mr. Rajan Kumar is the Managing Director of a Soap Manufacturing Company. To increase sales, the Board of Directors wanted to start a full-fledged marketing department. Mr. Kumar is entrusted with the task of finding a suitable candidate to head the proposed marketing department. After considering a number of candidates, he has narrowed down his choice to two persons: Viswanath Dutt and Rajnarain.

Mr. Viswanath Dutt has an excellent track-record in the company. During his fruitful association with the company, to be precise, ten years, he has always shown a high degree of enthusiasm and initiative in his work. He is still young (35 years) dynamic and aggressive. He is result oriented and is, naturally, more interested in ends rather than means. One of the workers, testifying his leadership qualities, remarked thus: "Though he is harsh at times, you will know where you stand when you work with him. When you have done a good job, he lets you know it." Mr. Dutt is willing to shoulder additional responsibilities. He decides things quickly and when action is required, he is always on his toes.

During his 15 years tenure in the company, Mr. Rajnarain has endeared himself to all his colleagues by his superior workmanship and pleasing manners. He always believes in the principle of employees participation in the decision-making process. Unlike Mr. Dutt he encourages his subordinates to come out with innovative ideas and useful suggestions. Before arriving at a decision he always makes it a point to consult his subordinates. Not surprisingly, all his subordinates are very pleased to work under him and praise his leadership qualities.

They readily admit that the participative climate has encouraged them to use their talents fully in the service of the organisation. Company records also bear evidence for the increase in the production soon after Rajnarain became the head of his department.

Questions:

(a) Analyse the leadership qualities and styles of Mr. Dutt and Rajnarain.

(b) Between the two people, who would you recommend for the position of a marketing manager?

Summary of the Case

Mr. Rajan Kumar, the Managing Director of a Soap Manufacturing Company was entrusted by the Board of Directors with the task of finding a suitable person for the position of a marketing manager. Mr. Kumar had shortlisted the persons. One Mr. Viswanath Dutt, a young person with ten years of experience and another Mr. Rajnarain with 15 years of service. A full-fledged marketing department had to be started by positioning a person as a marketing manager.

Problem of the Case

Whom to select, Dutt or Rajnarain, for the post of Marketing Manager was the problem of Mr. Rajan Kumar, the Managing Director.

(a) Analyse the leadership qualities and styles of Mr. Dutt and Rajnarain

Answer

Mr. Viswanath Dutt has a very good record of 10 years of service in a Soap Manufacturing Company. He has an interest and initiative in his work. He is dynamic, aggressive and young.

He is result oriented. He is for achievement of objectives by any methods. He is ready to accept any assignment. He takes decision quickly.

Mr. Viswanath is an aggressive leader. He is an autocratic leader. He possesses negative leadership style.

Mr. Rajnarain has 15 years of service in the company. He has superior workmanship, and good behaviour. He had participative power style. He invites suggestions and new ideas from his subordinates. He never takes unilateral decisions. He is liked by his subordinates. Under his headship, production increased.

Mr. Rajnarain is a positive leader. He follows participative power style. He is not an autocratic leader.

(b) Between the two people, who would you recommend for the position of a marketing manager?

Answer

I would recommend Mr. Rajnarain for the position of a marketing manager. Because leadership is the ability to persuade others to seek defined objectives enthusiastically. It is the human factor which binds a group together and motivates it towards goals. Leadership is something a person does, not something he has. There is an increase in the production soon after Mr. Rajnarain becomes the head of his department. Aggressiveness will not necessarily develop leadership with a group. As compared to Mr. Viswanath Dutt, Mr. Rajnarain is more suitable for the position of a marketing manager. He thinks of his company by giving consideration to means which is not the approach of Mr. Viswanath Dutt. An effective marketing manager should work closely with his subordinates. Hasty decision may create nasty situation. Hence, I recommend Mr. Rajnarain for the post of Marketing Manager.

Second Alternative answer for the Question (b)

I would recommend Mr. Viswanath Dutt for the position of a marketing manager. He has an excellent track-record in the company. He has high degree of enthusiasm and initiative in his work. He is young and dynamic. He is result oriented. He can shoulder additional responsibilities. He recognises a person when he does a good job. He takes quick decision and timely action. Hence Mr. Dutt is a better choice.

CASE NO. 3
CLASSIFYING MARKETS BY HOPES AND FEARS

Read the following case carefully and answer the questions given at the end.

The traditional method of analysing markets is to look at customer's age, sex, income, lifestyle or patterns of using products. People with certain age, sex and income tend to have some common habits and marketeers have concentrated on analysing these habits to develop their products. For banking and financial services companies, this classification doss not prove useful. Another way to classify consumers was developed which is based on people's hopes and fears.

A market research firm conducted extensive interviews with approximately 2500 people with bank accounts. The purpose of this study was to help banking institutions to attract public's spare cash with competitive rates for services offered. The study would also tell banks which customers to pursue and which to avoid.

The largest group of financial services customers is classified as planners and dealers. These customers are optimistic, well informed, fairly affluent and confident about their ability to handle their finances. These people are more interested in profit than convenience. They tend to spread their surplus among several investments. They shop around for the best deal and interested in getting maximum return. The financial services companies like banks must offer competitive rates and service charge to lure these customers. Since they are sophisticated they can evaluate themselves the alternative options. The banks, in this case, must convince them why their services are best for the cost charged to them.

The second group, the conservators, are confident but are cautious. They have saved their money through steady savings habits and made themselves sage. Thirty per cent of customers in this category are 55 or older. These customers want service, privacy and convenience. They usually maintain high balance and do their cheque cashing at the bank. They are not interested in automatic banking machines, banking by mail, or any other convenient services.

The first two groups account for 50 per cent of the customers. The third group, service seekers, 16 per cent of the market have less education, have lower incomes. The third group is also less sophisticated. Many of these (the third group) are widows. The top priority of service-seekers is not the biggest return on their money. They go to a bank because that is one of the few times in the day somebody services them.

The customers in the fourth category, 19 per cent of the market spend imprudently, believe in luck, not planning. They are pessimistic about the future. They are suspicious about bank's motives and are not concerned about bank services as it reminds them that they have very little savings. As many customers in this category have moderate incomes, they are not customers to be ignored.

The final category, about 12 per cent of the market, are called hopefuls. These customers dream that financial institutions may help them get a foothold on the slippery ladder of financial security. They consider bank credit as a stepping stone to enter into a suitable business or profession and secure firm settlement in their lives. Nearly half of them are between 18 and 35 years old. They are not aggressive. They have less education, and lower income than average. But they are eager to improve their financial status.

Summary of the Case

The banking and financial services companies have classified their customers on the basis of their hopes and fears. A market research firm conducted an interview programme with 2500 bank account holders. The objective of this study was to help bankers to attract people's spare cash with competitive rates for services offered, and to tell bankers which customers to pursue and which to avoid.

The largest group consists of planners and dealers. They shop around for the best deal and for maximum return in their deals. The financial services companies must offer competitive rates and service charge in order to attract these customers. The second group comprises of conservators. Thirty per cent of this group are older people. These customers want better service, privacy and convenience. The third group of people are service seekers, consisting of 16 per cent of the market, mostly widows. They are less educated, less sophisticated and lower income people. They are not for the biggest return on their money. The fourth category of customers are pessimists forming 19 per cent of the market. They are suspicious, with moderate incomes. But they cannot be ignored. The fourth group of customers are hopefuls who form 12 per cent of the market. They consider bank credit as a stepping stone to enter into a suitable business or profession. Half of these customers are between 18 and 35 years of age. They are less educated with lower income but they are eager to improve their economic condition.

This case is given for evaluating the usefulness of the market study conducted by the research firm, to suggest a better services package for attracting different groups of customers and to find out any other potential new group of customers.

Questions

1. Evaluate the usefulness of this market (segmentation) research study.

The market (Segmentation) research study helps to find out the needs, likes, dislikes, hopes and fears of the customers. It helps banking and financial companies to attract the public and to spare their cash with competitive rates for the services offered. The main intention of this type of research study is to remove the fears in the minds of the public and to attract the potential customers to deposit their spare cash with banks. Market research study is the way to classify the customer. Unlike the traditional method of analysing the market based on customer's age, sex, income, and lifestyle, the classification in banking and financial companies is based on customers, hopes and fears.

The market (segmentation) research study based on hopes and fears classifies the customers of banking and financial companies into the following types:

1. *Planners and dealers*

They are optimistic, well-informed, fairly affluent and confident about their ability to handle their financial resources. They give more emphasis on profit than convenience. They are interested in getting maximum return for their money.

2. *Conservators*

They are those people who are confident but cautious. Unlike planners and dealers, they emphasize more on better services, privacy and convenience. They want safety for their hard-earned money.

3. *Service seekers*

They comprise of low income groups, mostly widows. They are not interested in the high return for their money but they need better services from banking and financial companies.

4. *Pessimists*

They constitute 16 per cent of the market. Though they have moderate income, they spend imprudently. They are suspicious about banks' motives and are not concerned about bank services.

5. *Hopefuls*

This group consists of 12 per cent of the market. They consider bank credit as a stepping stone to enter into a suitable business and to come up in their life by improving their financial status.

Thus, by reading the minds of the customers with the help of research study, the banking and financial service companies are able to prepare better package so as to develop business by attracting these different segments of customers.

2. Assume that you are a bank manager. How would you prepare bank services package to attract business from these different segments of customers?

Assuming myself as a bank manager, I would prepare the following package to attract business from different segments of customers:

According to market (segmentation) research study based on hopes and fears, the customers of bank and financial service companies are classified into:

1. Planners and dealers
2. Conservators
3. Service seekers
4. Pessimists
5. Hopefuls.

In order to attract business from all the above mentioned segments of customers, I would prepare a bank service package which will cater the needs of different types of customers. For the first kind of customers, I will provide the required loan because customers of this category will handle their finances very prudently and confidently.

For them bank service is inevitable. They will repay the loan with interest without failure. Hence, for such customers, I will prepare a special programme. I will encourage them to start new industries or to expand their existing business units.

Since these customers are more interested in profits, I will give competitive return for their money invested in the bank.

For the second type of customers, I will provide them courteous service, and give care for their privacy and convenience.

Thirty per cent of customers in this category are 55 years old. They save their money through savings. Safety to their savings is a must. I will prepare a new attractive savings-package in order to attract fixed deposits. Cordial customer relation will be maintained. Customer meet programme will be introduced. Their grievances will be solved. Mail order transfer, quick service, etc., will be done to the satisfaction of these customers.

As a social obligation, I would cater the needs of service seekers. Goodwill will be created by offering better service to this type of customers. By giving small loans to the widows who are drawing family pension, I can light a lamp in their dark world and bring happiness to them. Widows will be given easy-instalment loan for buying tailoring machine or for starting household tiny business.

For the pessimists, the rules and regulations of the bank should be enlightened and their fear and suspicion should be eradicated. The importance of saving will be highlighted and the saving habit will be inculcated in their minds. They will be informed about the various programmes of the bank.

For the fifth category of customers, educational loan, end seed-capital loan will be provided which will push up their socio-economic status.

The needs of the hopefuls will be met by providing credit facilities at reasonable rate of interest. They will be encouraged to start small business. They will be educated to repay the loan which will help the bank to provide better credit facilities. This will improve their financial status and the growth of the bank.

Thus, I will prepare a package suitably to attract all the five segments of customers.

3. Is there another way to segment customers of financial services?

The market (segmentation) based on people's hopes and fears is the only way to segment customers of financial services. Hence, there is no other way to segment customers of financial services.

Alternative Answer

On the basis of income, the customers may be classified into high income, middle income, and low income. Accordingly suitable marketing strategy should be prepared. On the basis of occupation, the customers may be classified into primary sector customers, secondary sector customers and tertiary sector customers. Discriminatory policy may be followed to cater the needs of these types of customers.

CASE NO. 4
LINE AND STAFF RELATIONSHIP

After ten years of experience in various phases of personnel management in a large corporation, Harry Joans accepted a position as personnel manager in a small manufacturing firm located in a small city close to St Louis Missouri. Harry was tired of taking orders on every small details, as he was anxious to head an operation where he could introduce some innovative ideas. The owner of the firm had largely retired, leaving the everyday direction of the plant to George Wolfe. Harry and George got along very well and in the first year there was considerable progress in establishing better relations between the workforce and management.

Despite these advances, Harry was well aware of a labour union effort to organise the production force of some 200 employees. He took data periodically and was convinced that the greater bulk of employees would work for the union if given the chance. The treatment accorded to them by the owner and previous plant managers had built up substantial resentment which could not be quickly overcome by new policies. Harry also investigated the unions' organizing effort, and discovered that it was basically a well-managed and responsible organisation. As a consequence, he prepared a policy recommendation for the plant manager and owner. The essence of his position was that the firm should not make any move to forcefully oppose the union's effort. Upon reading this memorandum, the owner said, 'either he is for us or he is against us'. He instructed George to ask for Harry's resignation.

Question No. 1

What principle of lines and staff relationships is involved in this incident?

In the Line type of organisation, authority flows from the topmost executive to the bottom. The authority flows more or less in a straight line. The staff are experts who provide advice and service to the line officers. Their authority arises from their superior knowledge of a particular function. They do not have the power to command the line. In many organisations, the conflict between line and staff is a problem. The differences of opinion and conflict of interest between line and staff officers will defeat the very purpose of specialisation. It is very clear from the given case that the line and staff relationship in the organisation is strained from the very beginning which has led to resentment between the workers and the plant manager. Newman, Summer and Warren point out that duty (responsibility) authority and obligation (accountability) are the three inescapable features of delegation. In terms of authority, relationships line connotes authority to take action, authority to make decision, staff supplies facts and information that will enable the accountable manager to make the best decision. The principle of line and staff relationship involved in this incident is that of responsibility, authority and accountability.

The owner asks Harry to resign. It clearly shows that the owner is not willing to delegate authority to Harry.

Question No. 2

What values are being emphasized by the owner and by Harry?

The line and staff relationship is not cordial. The workers are waiting for an opportunity to oppose the management. They have developed a feeling of insecurity.

The owner is not for the introduction of any innovative ideas in his firm. The attitude of Harry is also not liked by the owner. The owner feels that Harry is against the management.

On the other hand, Harry is anxious to introduce some innovative ideas. He is for the formation of a union. He is willing to introduce new policies with the support of the union. He approaches the union positively. He says that the firm should not oppose the union. His ideas are not accepted by the owner. So he is asked to resign his position.

CASE NO. 5
DEFENSE DILEMMAS

Just three days after taking over as Crisp's president, Rajesh Srivastav was convinced that he ought to sound the alarm. For, he felt that the Chandigarh based leader in the Rs. 90 crore branded potato chips market had not woken up to the threat posed by the global brand, Snackies. Launched by the American soft-drinks giant, Cola King, Snackies had garnered a 25 per cent share of the market in just five years' time. Although Crisp's 12 per cent market-share meant that it was still ahead, what bothered Srivastav was that Snackies was scoring with younger consumers—the under-14s, who were setting the pace in chips consumption and were bound to be swayed by Cola King's global image. But was Srivastav right to be so worried about Snackies? Or did Crisp's real challenges lie elsewhere? Either way, what strategies could Srivastav adopt to ensure that Crisp gained a competitive edge for the future? SM Food's L.M. Agarwal, Contract Advertising's Shivjeet Kullar, and Empire Chemicals' Allan K. Saldanha debate the issue. With which of them do you agree?

Participants

Rajesh Srivastav, president, Anil Mathur, vice-president (marketing); Shyam Saxena; vice-president (operations); and Venkat Giri, vice-president (finance and administration).

Venue

Conference Room, Crisp Mahal, Chandigarh.

Srivastav:

GOOD AFTERNOON, GENTLEMEN

This is the first formal meeting of the executive committee since I joined Crisp as president three days ago. Let me begin with a few comments on the challenges before the company and what I believe should be its new priorities. Before I begin, I must state that I had been a Crisp-watcher for many years. Having been associated with the fast-moving consumer goods (FMCGS) market in the country for over two decades. I have seen the way Crisp has grown to become a market leader in branded potato chips.

What is noteworthy is that it has retained its leadership in the face of competition from Cola King, the American soft-drinks transnational, which launched its global snack-foods brand. *Snackies,* in 1991. I was going through the market-share figures recently. Crisp has a 70 per cent share of the market as compared to Snackies, whose share, six years after its launch, is 20 per cent. But, of course, the figures do not tell the truth. Product leadership, as you know, has two dimensions: share of market and share of mind. Crisp undoubtedly, enjoys a higher share of market, but Snackies is the leader as far as share of mind is concerned. You know that Snackies carries the glamour of global association with the consumer. Such appeal can give any brand a head-start although Snackies does not appear to have capitalised on that advantage.

But once you have a share of the consumers' mind, it becomes easy to improve upon marketshare consistently. I understand that Snackies had only 4 per cent of the market in the first year and increased it to 13 per cent in 1994. The fact, gentlemen, is that they are closing in slowly and steadily. It is this factor which poses the biggest challenge to Crisp. Our plans and priorities should be geared towards safeguarding our market-share and staving off further encroachment from Snackies. That's what I've set as my number one priority here.

Mathur: I think we all must agree that you have just about summed up the situation. Two months ago, we had commissioned impulse, the Delhi-based market research agency, to conduct a consumer survey in 25 large cities in northern India. The preliminary results, made available to us last week, reinforce your observation. Ask a consumer to name a branded potato chip—and the answer in 6 cases out of 10 is Snackies. Crisp has the largest number of satisfied customers—which is borne out by its market-share—but Snackies has some kind of aspirational value to it. And that is hardly good news for us. And let me update the data on market-shares, which isn't good either, it's 25 per cent for Snackies and 72 per cent for Crisp now. As you said, Snackies is closing in on Crisp. We can hardly afford to sit back and relax.

Srivastav: Thanks for that update, I must admit that my acquaintance with this business has so far been confined to munching potato chips once in a while. Anil why don't you brief me on the structure of the market?

Mathur: Shyam, would you like to sketch out the backdrop? After all, you've been with Crisp since its inception in 1987.

Saxena: Thanks, Anil. Welcome aboard, Rajesh. To begin at the beginning, it was in December 1984, that India witnessed the launch of the country's first packaged wafers brand. Golden

Crunch was launched by the Delhi based conglomerate. Indrajit Industries as part of its diversification into the food-processing business which, at that time, was perceived by many as having a growth potential. The company set up a fully automated plant—an investment for Rs. 8 crore—with the capacity to produce 400 kg of chips per hour from two tonnes of potato.

However, Golden Crunch has gone off the shelves since. In fact, we bought out the unit three years ago. It has been followed by 26 brands to date, many of which have since disappeared without a trace. Aloos Nik Naks, Lite Bite, Fun, Munch, Halo Popin, Heavenly Crunch, Tastee Twinkle, Winnies...lots of names. The mortality rate has been very high in this business. And whoever has survived has become a regional player with little impact at the all India level. The only brands with a national presence today are Crisp and Snackies.

Crisp came on the scene in 1987. There were three reasons for us to get into this business. First, with an annual output of 17 million tonnes, the country was then the fifth-largest producer of potatoes in the world. Secondly, more than 60 per cent of the cold-storage capacity of eight million tonnes in the country was devoted exclusively to potato. One could, therefore, buy potatoes in bulk when prices were low and sell the chips all year round. Finally, the Centre had identified food processing as a thrust area—in fact, it went on to set up a separate ministry for food processing—and offered subsidies and other fiscal concessions for new units. These were, of course, the macro-level reasons.

At the micro-level, the reasons were more compelling. As you are aware, Crisp was earlier known as Anand Vegetable Oils. Based in Chandigarh, the company had been manufacturing vanaspati since 1940. In the course of selling cooking oil to its target group of sweet shops, the company latched on to snack foods as a possible area of diversification in the mid-1980s. The snack-foods market in the country is valued at Rs. 1,500 crore per annum, of which potato wafers, as in all snack-foods markets worldwide, account far over 50 per cent.

Anand Vegetable Oils had a turnover of Rs. 7 crore in 1983 and suddenly we were looking at a market of about Rs. 800

crore. It was exciting. And, by coincidence, a chips-maker in the north was forced to make the distress sale of his plant. We bought the machinery for Rs. 3.50 crore—a price that cut our capital costs by nearly 70 per cent. That gave us a head-start in a business where control of the Total Delivery Cost (TDC) is critical not only for profitability, but also for sheer survival.

Giri: May I clarify this point? One reason for failure in the packaged chips business is the lack of understanding of the concept of TDC. Potatoes are available at less than Rs. 10 per kg. and a 50 gm packet of chips, packed in an attractive trilaminate bag retails, at Rs. 10 which works out to Rs. 200 per kg. This gives an illusion of attractive margins. Besides, there are no entry barriers. It is a low investment, low-tech business. But it is also a business of low margins—less than 3 per cent, in fact—particularly if you are a major national player. Your expenditure on transportation, distributor commissions, and packaging often goes haywire. Unless they are monitored closely they can distort the cost revenue balance badly.

Mathur: Another point of interest is that our real competition comes from the unorganised sector, where the volume of business—at Rs. 750 crore—is 10 times that of branded chips. The sector comprises innumerable *halwais* operating in every nook and corner of the country. They buy cheap and stale potatoes, fry them in oil of dubious quality, and sell the wafers in loose polythene bags at about Rs. 40 per kg. The product is greasy, messy, soggy and unhygienic besides having a different taste and offering little variety in terms of flavours. That's a weakness. We have tried to exploit by ensuring high qualify raw materials, and fresh and tangy chips in air-tight packs. But this is still a price-sensitive business. Value for Money is more important than a premium image or even product quality. For a firm aiming at long-term brand-building, this is both an entry-barrier and a great opportunity.

Giri: But when consumer expectations are low, it is often difficult to establish product differentiation. Unlike a majority of FMCG products, the scope for brand positioning and premium pricing is limited for potato chips. Your success depends on how well you manage the TDC, and how effectively you handle distribution. Freight is a major cost component which makes the decentralisation of manufacturing operations an important issue. Production centres should be close to consumption centres, that is why the markets are regionalised. In fact, a bulk of the consumption of potato chips is confined to parts of North India because that is where most plants are located. The way I see it, the only route through which we can grow the potato chips business is the franchisee route. This is a strategic issue that we should examine.

Srivastav: But Giri, apart from keeping TDC under control, I think yet another factor critical to survival in the snack foods business is regular line extensions.

Mathur: True consumers are constantly looking for new experiences of taste and are prone to experiment with innovative flavours. We have eight flavours today—as opposed to Snackies five—of which the three core flavours account for over 85 per cent of turnover. The others are being retained, even if they incur losses, in order to ensure shelf-space and sustain awareness with the consumer. Line extensions, however, critical for survival, carry their own costs. Equally important are advertising and promotion. We had a turnover of Rs. 45 crore last year, on which we made profits of Rs. 2 crore. This was because we spent over Rs. 8 crore on advertising. Snackies spent Rs. 10 crore on advertising on a turnover of Rs. 12 crore. However, it can afford to sustain losses because it is part of a $3.30 billion transnational group.

There are a few other issues that the impulse survey has thrown up. First, although we have three different pack sizes—50 gm, 100 gm and 200 gm—it is the 50 gm pack, which retails at Rs. 12, that consumers find "handy and convenient". This is surprising, because the other two packs are priced lower—the 100 gm packet Rs. 22 and the 200 gm pack at Rs. 40. Secondly, the market is being increasingly driven by the teenage segment, with 65 per cent of the consumption of potato chips accounted for by the under-14 age-group. This is clearly an area of risk for us. Crisp is positioned as the ultimate family snack: for everybody from grandparents to grandchildren for all occasions. Cola King is perceived the world over as a new generation drink, and Snackies can easily latch on to that platform to cover a huge chunk of the market. Our own advertising lacks a pivot.

Srivastav: That's a very valid point. Before we take it up further, may I ask each of you for your ideas on what our priorities for action should be? That will give this discussion some focus.

Saxena: Franchising that should be the vehicle of market expansion—not the expensive route of capacity creation. The proportion of fixed costs is low in our business. So, sooner or later, you will reach a situation where the more you produce, the more you lose per unit. There are only two ways in which you can handle this. Control TDC or franchise your operations. Franchising also ensures savings on freight. And if at all there is need for a new plant—under the pressure of increasing demand two or three years down the line—it should be located close to a major consumption centre.

Mathur: You know, one major problem is that eating chips is considered an indulgence in our country. It's guilt-ridden, and not a wholly pleasurable activity. This is mainly because of the misguided impression that chips add calories. As the market leader, Crisp should take some initiatives in setting the record straight through some aggressive promotions. Potato is, after all, healthy. It is rich in vitamins and proteins. We have evidence to prove that 200 gm of unfried potatoes can provide half the daily requirements of Vitamin C. To show our concern for consumer health, we could launch low-fat versions or develop a reduced cooking-oil process, and even prove how it is cleaner and more hygienic than what is sold by the road-side vendor. The second area of strategic concern is the risk involved in a single-product focus. I think we should diversify into salted snacks and nankeens.

Giri: You mentioned, Rajesh, that line extensions are critical for survival. But I would be wary of extending a line merely to increase brand awareness. Mathur talked of the hidden costs of line extensions. We did some studies last year, and I have data to prove that the unit cost of a multi-flavour line can be 40 per cent higher than the cost of producing only the most popular item in the line. So, line extensions should be a careful exercise. Secondly, we have about eight lakh retailers all over the country, and our retail margins, at 40 per cent, are high. I think this is a cost which should be benchmarked with, say, a cigarette manufacturing company.

Srivastav: Thank you very much for your ideas gentlemen. You have given me plenty to chew on. May I suggest we meet again in a week's time? Meanwhile, could each of you prepare a short memo for my benefit, outlining these ideas? We can take it from there.

Does Crisp actually face a threat from Snackies? If so, how should the company consolidate its leadership position? And how can it influence the structure of the potato chips market to gain a competitive edge in the business?

Solution A

By *Allan K. Saldanha,* CEO, Empire Chemicals

The situation faced by Crisp is no different from what any Indian FMCG company experiences with the entry of

THE SWOT

	Strengths	Opportunities
1.	Has a 70% share of the branded potato chips market.	Could wean the consumer away from unbranded products.
2.	A relatively wide and deep system of distribution.	Could expand the market by appointing franchisees.
3.	Eight flavours, with the top three accounting for 85% of sales.	Could segment the market through line extensions.
	Weaknesses	**Threats**
1.	Product carries negative associations, such as gulit.	Transnational rivals gaining market share relatively rapidly.
2.	Limited possibility of product differentiation in this category.	Prime competitors attaining top of mind awareness.
3.	Little scope for premium pricing in a competitive market place.	Managing total delivery costs, and margins, becoming tougher.

transnationals. The good news for Crisp is that it has successfully pushed out domestic brands, consolidating its position. Yet, the threat to Crisp is real. Particularly because transnationals like Cola King can afford to underwrite losses from say, one product line. Crisp should, therefore, adopt a two-pronged approach containment of competition and market development.

Crisp will have to improve the depth and the width of its distribution. The efficient servicing of retail outlets should be a matter of priority as should be the control of TDC. Since net margins in this business are not high, any laxity could adversely impact the bottomline. Further, morale of the salesforce must be maintained at a high level. These are all part of the ongoing battle for survival and supremacy. In the long-term, Crisp will have to address three issues that are critical for growth and profitability. It should tap the huge unbranded potato chips market. It should address the teenage segment—particularly the under 14s—more effectively. And it should take steps to remove misconceptions about the consumption of potato.

For a product like potato chips, which is characterised by low bulk density, transportation over long distances is not cost-effective. Third-party manufacture at multiple locations and franchising makes better sense. The former entails greater company investment in storage and distribution; the latter requires tight over quality standards. Crisp should choose the franchisee route for market development. It can take on the supply of raw materials like potatoes, cooking oil, flavours, and packaging materials, confining the role of a franchisee to frying, flavouring, and packaging. This strategy will enable Crisp to develop independent entrepreneurs, and ensure the most-cost-effective delivery to the consumers.

Crisp should also take fresh look at its brand positioning. Actual consumption points to the neglect of the under-14 age-group, and Crisp should, therefore, strengthen its presence here even while drawing in more from other segments. Sub branding is worthwhile here, something like the Scholar's Pack or the Scholar's Mini-Meal. Below-the-line promotions in support of this concept should help to bring about the focus that advertising needs. Consumer education campaigns are another dimension of market development. Of course, if special processing technologies are available to ensure low oil pick-up, fears in the minds of calorie-conscious consumers will be greatly minimised. Crisp can also take an aggressive marketing stand by introducing "formed chips", on the lines of Bahlsen of Germany, which has all the advantages of low oil, economy in packaging, and longer shelf life.

A subtle campaign against oil-soaked, farsan-shop-variety potato chips can lead to an awareness of the benefits of branded chips. In fact, Crisp should initiate—with the help of state agricultural departments—an awareness campaign to educate people about the benefits of potato, perhaps, on the line 5 of the egg promotion campaign. After all, the fortunes of the company are linked to potato. In this context, I feel that Crisp should be wary of entering the namkeens market because the market is not organised. Although the individual buying preference seems to be tipped in favour of 50 gm packets, delineating the various Crisp packs as family packs, party packs, and institutional packs (targeted at bulk users like hotels and corporate canteens) could also be looked at. In the ultimate analysis, it may be worthwhile examining the options of a strategic alliance with Snackies Thums Up and Coke.

Solution B

By *Shivjeet Kullar*, Creative Director, Contract Advertising.

Faced with slowly growing or stagnating markets in their land of origin, gigantic transnational brands are eyeing the Indian market for further growth. Their chiefs, donning the robes of corporate Genghiz Khans, are in search of new lands to conquer. To this end, their first target is, obviously, successful Indian brands. At all costs, they want to buy them out, think them out, and take them out. And to achieve this, they can reach into their deep pockets. In this case, a $3.30 billion enterprise can throw millions into the fray. Consider the most recent examples. Thums Up sold out to the Coca-Cola juggernaut, Kwality threw in its lot with Wall's. Zee entered into an alliance with STAR TV and is now on the verge of being knocked off the edge. The prospects are quite chilling for Crisp.

However, let us look at the brighter side of things. Mr. Crisp is obviously, a very canny and savvy marketeer. Not only has he held his own against the overseas battalions for six long years, he has had the foresight to realise that he cannot afford to be complacent even though he has repulsed the first, second, and third waves of attack. And herein lies the answer to what Crisp needs to do. Despite the fact that it is an overwhelming leader, it should change its strategy from defence to attack. Because the truth is that while it is possible to gain ground against a guarded leader, it is virtually impossible to catch a leader who is on the move. A great example of this is Colgate. Just when the other brands thought they knew what they should do against it, Colgate would go ahead and do something totally new. So that is exactly what Crisp should do.

Let us look at what Crisp should do at two levels—general-vision level and specific-threat level. At the former, Crisp should become as unexpected and innovative as possible. Is it possible to have the whole country searching for "golden" chips because one pack of Crisp in a thousand has a thin gold coin inside it? Can there be a double-flavoured surprise pack that tastes like nothing the consumer has ever tasted before? How about a little napkin stapled to each pack sold at cinema halls? What about a party pack that comes along with party music? Or a dealer display contest, where the winning dealer will have his or her photograph printed on the first one lakh packs of Crisp manufactured in a month? Basically the excitement from Crisp should be non-stop. Of a promotion and marketing budget of, say, Rs. 10 crore, Crisp should set aside 20 per cent for NBDBS (Never Been Done Befores).

Now, at a specific level, what is the most important issue that Crisp needs to address? Well, to overstate the point, Crisp has the present, but Snackies seems to have the future. Because, while Crisp is a likeable catch-all brand. Snackies seems to appeal to the younger, trendier lot. As the Indian consumer profile becomes more sophisticated—and there is growing evidence to this effect—Snackies is bound to gain. So Crisp needs to do something about this. The scenario is, however, a little tricky. Why? Crisp should catch the younger customers without alienating the present ones. In other words, devise a way to appeal to Pappu, Bittoo, Sanju and Chimpu without omitting papa, mama, nana, nani and the chhota baby. This is classic problem often faced by marketeers. Obviously, the answer for Crisp is not to put on a mental mini skirt overnight; it might end up losing its mass appeal. And if that happens, Crisp will be in deep trouble.

However, that does not mean that there are no choices. If Crisp has, say, eight flavours, it could select three of the more unusual ones and market them under a sub-brand, such as Crisp Zany. This sub-brand could then be advertised to target the younger generation. It should be advertised on the popular channels on satellite television and in youth magazines. The message can be Westernised, stylish, and glamorous. Crisp Zany could draw strength and support from the mother brand, and yet be different—just as Colgate Dental Cream and Colgate Gel are so different in terms of their brand image. To start with, Crisp Zany may not bring in large volumes, but it is an investment for the future.

Solution C

By *L.M. Agarwal* Executive Director, SM Foods

Yes, Crisp Does Face a Threat from snackies. But this should not worry Crisp too much as there are more markets and consumers to be tapped in order to maintain sales volumes. The threat from Snackies, as is rightly believed, is due to its international appeal and optimum pricing, which are providing the consumer with the motivation to relocate their preferences. This factor will soon see more consumers moving to Snackies. This is the expected and natural outcome in a competitive market.

Crisp held the No. 1 position in the country as it was the only large-scale manufacturer with the advantage of maintaining a control on the TDC of chips. This was because its other operations were supported by a good product and innovative marketing. With international competition stepping in, it is natural for the consumer to try out new brands and even shift loyalty. This would be considered absolutely normal in any international market. Here begins the marketing game, and how you play makes the difference.

The question of how Crisp should ward off an attack is something which needs a lot of inputs, like checking out consumer attitudes, preferences and changing needs. Basically, Crisp needs to consolidate its existing position and concentrate on its prime market rather than go in for width, which comes with additional costs and low contributions. Franchising is something which is not going to be cost effective initially, but is definitely worth a try as this will solve the problems of distance and cost of freight.

But franchising is not going to work unless it is able to convince some of its old stockists and dealers to invest in plant and machinery. A 200 kg per hour capacity plant requires an investment of Rs. 2 crore in addition to the recurring costs of raw materials, manpower, packaging, plant maintenance and other overheads. Since franchising merely requires the principal to collect royalty on counter sales—by lending its brandname and ensuring product quality through conformity to pre-determined standards—how many stockists would be willing to make an investment on their own? Very few. And Crisp would find its own costs of operations going haywire if it were to foot the bill.

That is the basic problem in the branded potato chips business. The competitive edge will come with the capacity to handle the pressure during the present price war, which will ultimately determine who is going to be the king. In the process, Crisp should watch out and not get too deeply embeded in the sand. What Srivastav and his team should examine are the strengths and weaknesses of the brand, the company and its sales personnel. They should later work on a strategy of brand-building and consumer motivation, which are the two most important elements in keeping a brand alive in the trade. Growth and profits will follow.

CASE NO. 6
BOSS-SUBORDINATE RELATIONS

Mr. Jame an MBA in his early fifties, an administrator occupying the number two position in the hierarchy of a large organisation, had a number of junior level managers under him. He also had in the hierarchy, a couple of supervisors/inspectors (both male and female) and a number of junior assistants working under him. A jovial person, Mr. Jame was keen on the application of his formal education in management and innovative techniques; and therefore, he used to move freely with his subordinates and colleagues. Firm but fair, tough but tender, were his mottos. He was recently transferred to a place where orthodoxy still persisted.

Some of the junior assistants in the new set up were extremely intelligent and compensated for the average intelligence of the supervisor. Any important work assigned to Mr. Jame was completed successfully with their help.

Mr. Jame noticed a changed pattern of behaviour in his supervisors and was concerned about it. When he tried to probe the reasons behind it, he was surprised to know that it stemmed from his own casual behaviour with the staff. It was felt that his language was too familiar (in case of ladies, it conveyed a misconception of closeness; and with men, it was perceived as disrespect).

The matter reached his boss also. The boss, who was his well-wisher pointed out that he should change his pattern of behaviour. Mr. Jame replied that the approach he used with youngsters, peers and older people was one of affection, familiarity and deference, respectively. He further argued that he did not stand on formalities arising from his position in the office. Unfamiliarity with the language and ambiguity regarding the usage of words were other factors he quoted as reasons for the present dilemma. Moreover, colleagues who were jealous of Mr. Jame were fanning the ill-feeling, he felt.

Regardless of anything, the boss advised Mr. Jame to mend his behaviour stating that the Western techniques of 'Personnel Management' which incorporates free mingling with the subordinates and developing a spirit of camaraderie between the boss and the subordinate, will not work in the Indian situation. However, Mr. Jame countered that the existing pattern of boss-subordinate relationship in the Indian situation should be changed to benefit the organisation. The boss did not agree with his views and advised him to change his pattern of working. Mr. Jame was also told to deal with the junior assistants and supervisors, etc., only through the junior managers and never directly, as this practice dilutes authority and encourages indiscipline.

Mr. Jame changed his pattern, by avoiding the regional language and also addressing everyone in the most respectful tone. He started calling the junior managers even for minute matters.

Some of the staff who used to like Mr. Jame were upset due to his changed behaviour and were trying to keep away from him resulting in less productivity and turnover in the organisation.

Colleagues who were jealous of Mr. Jame started pointing out to the boss that Mr. Jame was becoming inefficient and attributed to negligence. When Mr. Jame came to know of this, he offered to quit. The boss was perplexed. So were the staff.

Consider these questions:

1. How can the situation be improved? With whom do you agree, Mr. Jame or his boss?
2. Was Mr. Jame justified in changing his attitude, acting upon the advice of the boss?

First Analysis

Supervisors need training

New management techniques are employed to attain set objectives or to tackle specific problems of the organisation. Success results only if the technique used is relevant to the subject and is implemented properly, keeping in consonance with environmental factors like culture, tradition, language and attitude of the people.

In this case, Mr. Jame motivated junior assistants to use their skills to successfully complete their assignments. But in the process, he did not involve his supervisors who felt neglected and insecure. As Mr. Jame was very successful as far as work was concerned, the supervisors could not complain to the management in that respect. Instead, as it happens in most such cases, supervisors, diverting the issue, complained about his behaviour thereby venting their frustration. Neither Mr. Jame nor his boss analysed the situation in-depth to find out the actual problem. This resulted in failure, after Mr. Jame changed his behaviour pattern following the advice of his boss.

It is a good practice to motivate lower level staff to apply initiative, perception and skills on the job, but in order to achieve success, motivation and participation has to encompass all levels of hierarchy in an organisation.

To improve the situation in this case, some of the supervisors should be trained to understand the concepts of joint participation like quality circles, joint councils, etc. Efforts should be made to implement the same thereby giving an opportunity to everyone to participate in the work and progress of the organisation.

Second Analysis

Unproductive compromise

Mr. Jame's principle of 'firm but fair' and 'tough but tender' is perfectly commendable. Egoism kindles animosity. On the other hand, the tenacity and tenderness of an officer can galvanize the hidden spirit of co-operation, even in an obstinate subordinate. In many offices, quite a few officers are nominal and serve as mere ornaments to the chairs, they can be classified as deadwood. There are others who apply charm and sycophancy to stick to their chairs. Such people try to eclipse the efficacy of their juniors in order to splash their names in the limelight Mr. Jame's direct rapport with the junior assistants not only testifies to the veracity of the responsibilities shouldered by the latter, but also exposes the inefficiency of the intermediate supervisors.

Mr. Jame's transfer to the conservative environment had helped him to lay bare the loopholes existing in the new set up. Though Mr. Jame vindicated his principles strongly, he compromised by changing his attitude to appease his boss, which in the long run proved unproductive.

Deviation from his rooted principles for survival, has worked to his detriment in the long run and his decision to quit is a direct offshoot of his earlier action.

To improve the situation, the following steps are suggested:

1. The nominal officers who live in the shade of their subordinates must be weeded out or put to acid test to gauge their worth and, if found suitable, they should be utilised properly.
2. Flexibility should be the prerogative of top administrators.
3. Hard work should be recognised and rewarded at the correct time.
4. Avenue should be opened for zealous and intelligent staff to prove their merit.

Third Analysis

Moderation—The key word

Despite Mr. Jame's innovative and positive management techniques and his enthusiasm to apply them in real practice, something still went wrong, in so far as his relations with his people were concerned. Applying theoretical management techniques to work situations is good, but the approach should change from situation to situation. The method succeeded in Mr. Jame's earlier assignment but failed in an orthodox environment.

In a working environment, it is not enough to be good—one must also appear to be so. This is an important aspect of internal public relations which cannot be overlooked. The supervisors might have felt a little alienated for obvious reasons. Mr. Jame should have moderately adjusted his behaviour and manner of working to bring in the necessary changes gradually. Bypassing supervisors is not generally recommended although following strict hierarchy or compartmentalisation in a work situation reduces the efficiency and tells upon the productivity.

It is always better to carry the whole team together. Where men and women are working together, one has to be a little cautious in our society to ensure that working together does not lead to misconceptions as has happened in Mr. Jame's case.

Mr. Jame seems to have viewed the entire episode emotionally. Group behaviours and situations have to be understood in the right perspective. An informal meeting between Mr. Jame, his supervisory, and junior staff might help to remove the communication gaps. There was no need for any drastic or major change in Mr. Jame's attitude. While following the advice of his boss, he should have taken the hint in the right perspective and applied the change with moderation to suit the purpose.

Fourth Analysis

Please all and you please none

The problems depicted here are very common. Mr. Jame was a jovial person, well accepted in his former set up. In the new set up, he appears to have been depending on a few intelligent juniors and it is likely that this could have been misunderstood as favouritism. The misconceptions regarding his manner of behaviour might have been perpetuated by a dissatisfied and jealous group of employees. The advice of Mr. Jame's boss that the former should change his approach, is not correct. The assumption that western techniques cannot work in India is also not correct. Mr. Jame should continue with his style of operation, with proper care to handle dissatisfied persons separately, one by one and sort out the problems. By changing his own attitude he had annoyed even those who have been with him and this has created total confusion. A true boss is one who can mould his subordinates to his style of operations. In any case, it is never possible to please all. In an organisation, there cannot be a predefined method of solving problems. They are to be taken individually and solved, based one's own previous experience and intuition.

Fifth Analysis

Do not quit

When Mr. Jame's boss has delegated authority to Mr. Jame, he is perfectly justified in suggesting that the way in which he behaves with his junior executives and supervisors may not set a healthy trend in the organisation.

The fact that some of the junior assistants are more intelligent than the supervisors, does not give Mr. Jame the right to bypass managers and supervisors, until and unless the latter's inefficiency is proved. Breaking the chain of hierarchy without proper justification may end in failure.

Mr. Jame followed the right course by complying with his boss's advice to change his attitude. But this change should not be allowed to affect his productivity. He should fix targets for completion of duties assigned to the junior managers, and only if they fail to achieve them, he should approach the junior assistants directly. Further, Mr. Jame should keep his boss fully informed about this line of action, to steer clear of trouble, in future.

Internal squabbles and jealousies are inevitable in any organisation. Mr. Jame should not allow them to reflect on his performance. His offer to quit is an indication of failure. He should try to come to terms with the situation and steer it in his favour.

Sixth Analysis

Carte blanche

It is a very difficult task to change one's work pattern and behaviour overnight. In the present set up, as the junior assistants are extremely intelligent Mr. Jame is justified in adopting 'Western Techniques' as far as the boss-subordinate relationship is concerned. Mr. Jame's language may not be appreciated by some people. However, most of the subordinates adore him and perform their respective duties leading to higher productivity. A sudden vicissitude in Mr. Jame's behaviour led to the feeling among the sincere subordinates that Mr. Jame was trying to exercise his authority in dealing with the former and hence, they drifted away from him.

I agree with Mr. Jame as he was performing his duties with utmost sincerity and was able to extract optimum productivity from his subordinates. Mr. Jame's boss should not be misled by the jealousies of other employees. A boss should always concern himself about the output and sincerity of his subordinate and not about his way of functioning. The situation can best be improved, if the boss does not pay heed to the jealous colleagues of Mr. Jame and gives a carte blanche to the latter to perform his duties.

Mr. Jame is not justified in changing his attitude which resulted in (i) misunderstanding; (ii) subordinates keeping away from him; and (iii) less productivity and turnover in the organisation.

Though it is widely believed that 'The Boss is always right'. Mr. Jame should have prevailed over his boss to accept his present mode of behaviour in this case.

CASE NO. 7
WAGE ADMINISTRATION

Deductions and Interpersonal Relations

A large public sector undertaking employing thousands of supervisors got an interim injunction order from the High Court in a case represented by the Employees Union regarding calculation of tax. The stay order was not to take into account City Compensatory Allowance (CCA), Dearness Allowance (DA) and Additional Dearness Allowance (ADA) for calculation of net taxable income. If this stay order was implemented/made applicable to that section of the employees who were members of the Union, most of the staff will be out of the tax net. The matter was brought to the notice of the General Manager by the Accounts Department for advice/orders. The General Manager contacted his close friend and associate, a senior incometax department official, who advised him, to persuade the staff and to take into account CCA, DA and ADA for calculation of net taxable income and to recover tax from all the employees as due irrespective of the High Court interim injunction or irrespective of the Union to which they belong. The justification for this advice was that the Direct Taxes Amendment Bill was being passed and that in any case the tax will have to be recovered inclusive of CCA, DA and ADA. The General Manager though reluctant, felt that the advice of his friend should be heeded. The matter was taken to the Personnel Department. The Chief of Personnel held a different view. His view was that the CCA, DA and ADA should not be included in taxable income for the following reasons:

1. They are the High Court's interim orders and if not obeyed there may be a contempt petition by the Union.
2. When in doubt, we should always await the final outcome.
3. If we calculate net taxable income without taking CCA, DA and ADA we are not only not violating the High Court's orders but also the staff will feel that we are one with them and not anti labour.
4. The Union will feel happy, since the others who are not members of the Union, can be wooed and they now know the prowess of the Union.

When this was pointed out to the General Manager, he again contacted the income tax official. The official stated that the Amendment Bill is in final stage and is almost passed and it would, therefore, be wise to recover the full tax taking into account the CCA, DA and ADA to avoid double work and extra labour. The Chief of Personnel did not agree with this view and added that considering the economics of present day with the rising trend in price index, etc., an amount which is not clearly recoverable at present and in doubt but, will become recoverable subsequently should not be recovered now. It should be recovered only later when it becomes clearly due and recoverable. Moreover, this course of action would show to the workers the organisations, good intentions towards their workers, oneness with the staff, abiding law and the impression than we care for the Union, though this may involve additional labour and extra work later on. The Chief of Personnel also pointed out that employee/employer relation is always pay 'now', recover 'later' and the maximum payments due—first preference, recoveries due—in due course would always create a better industrial climate particularly in the context of our culture and work ethos coupled with the socialistic concept of the Government. It would also be good for the organisation, he argued.

The General Manager was perplexed not only because the high official of the tax department was a well-wisher and good friend of the General Manager and his advice was valued, but also in the interest of the company, he did not want strained relations with the tax department.

Question: With whom do you agree and why? If you are the General Manager how would you deal with the situation?

First Analysis

Personnel man is right

The Chief of Personnel's view that CCA, DA and ADA should not be included in taxable income is perfectly justified.

Sincerity is the guiding principle for maintaining cordial industrial relations. If the management, following the income tax official's advice, deducts tax, taking into account CCA, DA and ADA also, the workers might feel that management is finding ways to avoid payment to workers.

The question of double work does not arise because this work is a part and parcel of the organisation's routine. How can a Bill which has been introduced but not passed be construed as a law? Indeed, there are standing instructions of the High Court to the contrary.

Even if one can persuade the workers to accept such a move, what is the guarantee that the Amendment Bill will be passed in the Parliament? Particularly so, in the face of numerous instances where the government is forced to withdraw Bills after their introduction, due to various reasons.

Such a move is sure to spoil interpersonal relations. The General Manager should not consider the advice of the tax official who has no exposure to human relations in organisations. He should go by the advice given by a professional personnel man who is well-versed in human relations.

Second Analysis

Earn Goodwill

Even though a Bill is in the final stage, it cannot be substituted for an Act and enforced. Any action in contravention to the stay order of the High Court tantamounts to contempt of Court. It is, therefore, safer to comply with the stay order for the present and deduct the said allowances as and when the amended Act comes into force. In any case, the Company is not going to incur any loss. On the contrary, the Company will certainly earn the goodwill of the employees if it does not deduct from the allowances now. Had I been the General Manager, I would have fully endorsed the views of the Chief of Personnel without referring the issue to the income tax official.

Third Analysis

Deposit the Money

In view of the High Court injunction order, the advice of income tax official cannot be accepted. The interim injunction order is a legal and enforceable order. Amendment Bill will be enforceable only when it becomes an Act.

Had I been the General Manager I would have explained to the Union, through the Chief of Personnel, that Direct Tax Amendment Bill will become an Act very soon, whereupon CCA, DA, etc., will be taken into account for the purpose of calculation of tax. The staff will be out of the tax net only temporarily. Therefore, the Union should retain the amount equivalent to income tax with the Company as a deposit which will go to them if they win the case. If they lose the case, it will be deposited in the treasury.

CASE NO. 8
ROLE RIGIDITY

'Inside Rails' is an organisation with a couple of thousands of employees. The organisation is headed by a Managing Director-President with a number of Vice Presidents for each department—like engineering, accounts, mechanical, personnel, etc. The Vice President-Personnel is the co-ordinating head for that department with two Executive Directors one each for dealing with administration and policy and the other for industrial relations. The Executive Director for administration has a Director to help him at the policy level, though for certain purposes of administration, the Director is vested with independent powers by delegation. The Executive Director-Industrial Relations has a couple of officers to help him to deal with the Union matters as also the legal aspects of the Company. The Executive Director-Industrial Relations is to co-ordinate meetings with the Managing Director and the Unions accountable to the Managing Director and answerable to Unions with regard to agreements, etc.

The Vice President-Personnel, one day, received a note from the Executive Director-Industrial Relations that the Director-Personnel has been indifferent to industrial relations problems of the company, he has been irregular in attending to the Union meetings, not at all attended one of the important meetings fixed by the Executive Director-Industrial Relations. The Vice President simply marked it to Executive Director-Administration. The Executive Director-Administration gave a copy of that note to Director-Personnel and called for his explanation by a specified date. The Director-Personnel, a qualified and experienced personnel man, called on the Executive Director-Administration and tried to discuss the matter, but the Executive Director wanted a written explanation from the Director!

The Vice President came to Personnel Department, by choice, while the Executive Director-Industrial Relations and Executive Director-Administration from other departments are on deputation on a stop gap arrangement. The Director-Personnel felt very unhappy and hurt over the manner in which the whole episode was dealt with, nonetheless, he explained in writing that he had not been irregular in attending the meetings when called for as could be seen from records and that it was because of prefixed engagement of "selection" to select a huge number of employees for a higher post from amongst the large number of employees attending from all over the State, that he could not attend the suddenly fixed meeting with the Union. He also counselled and sounded a word of caution that unless there is better camaraderie and understanding particularly in the Personnel aspects which are 'human centered', the organisational goal will be defeated. The Director also felt harassed and offered to quit. The Executive Director-Administration passed on this explanation to Vice President-Personnel.

The Director later understood that on that particular day, when he was busy with the selection, the Executive Director-Industrial Relations had asked the Executive Director-Administration to attend the meeting in place of the Director and Executive Director-Administration had regretted. Though the Assistant to Director ably handled the situation, the Executive Director-Industrial Relations was feeling let down.

The questions that arise from this case are:

1. Did this situation arise on account of the inexperience of Executive Director-Personnel?
2. Is there any mishandling of the situation?
3. Could there be Director's indifference?
4. Was it right on the part of Executive Director-Industrial Relations to have given a note to Vice President against the Director—even though it may have been directed against the Executive Director-Administration?
5. Was it right on the part of the Vice President to have escalated the matter by marking the note to Executive Director-Administration?
6. Was it right on the part of Executive Director-Administration to have called for the explanation of the Director who was the qualified experienced personnel man available in the organisation?

7. How far the Director was justified in his offering to quit the organisation?

Is there an organisational overlap?

Analysis

This is a case of inter- and intra-personal conflicts

A small intra-personal conflict assumes the geometrical proportions of inter-personal conflict by mishandling. The whole episode smacks of ego to identify conflict. The episode would not have at all taken place, if there was empathy. The Vice President could have diffused the situation by a discussion avoiding unnecessary paper work. Because of the exchange of notes, the conflicts between the tops have surfaced to the 'subordinates' level.

Inter-personal conflicts can be attributed to various causes. Inter-personal conflicts may, sometimes, be due to organisational overlap but they occur mainly due to non-existence of empathy. Empathy is the ability to understand another person's frame of mind and accept it—not necessarily agree with it. By being empathetic, productive interaction takes place. Genuine empathy (as distinct from being 'empathetic for short-term goals') ensures trust and confidence.

The other important cause is 'ego' or 'super ego' problems. Authority erosion or role reduction does not seem to play any vital role in intra-personal conflict. If inter-personal conflicts are to be avoided—particularly in personnel, one should always be positively empathetic. One should work in a state of 'deflated ego' if not in a state of 'egoless ego' as a Manager.

There is no organisational overlap. The Director should point out the shortcomings to the Vice President instead of quitting.

CASE NO. 9
ILLEGAL STRIKE AND LOCK-OUT

A large workshop of a public utility service, engaged in the manufacture of spare parts as well as in repairing, had a strength of 3,000 workers and was headed by a Chief Mechanical Engineer (CME) who in turn was assisted by a Personnel

Officer-cum-Welfare Officer (PO). Works Manager (WM), Production Engineer (PE) and a band of Assistant Works Managers (AWM). There were about eight sections, each dealing with a particular type of work, the end product being the manufactured/repaired vehicles.

The workshop being in its infancy, the working was generally normal and excepting exchange of harsh words, heated arguments between the management, supervisors and workmen, sometimes, there was hardly any untoward incident. Suddenly, on a working day, during the first shift, after the Chief Mechanical Engineer/Works Manager, took a round, they were informed that the workers had become restive. The workmen, after adopting go slow tactics for sometime had struck work and were sitting idle in groups. They had switched off the machines. Earlier, on that day, the workmen had punched their cards at 7.00 a.m. as usual and reported for work at 7.10 a.m. Nothing was unusual till 7.45 a.m. when the Works Manager, etc., were on usual round. But by 8.25 a.m. everything seemed to have gone wrong. On receipt of the information the CME, WM and PO went round the workshops asking the workmen the reasons and appealing to them to resume work. No reply was forthcoming from any corner, nor did the workmen resume work.

A notice was then circulated appealing to workmen to resume work and indicating that the system of 'no work, no pay' would come into force. This too had little effect.

The CME/WM reported the matter to the top management, stating *inter alia* that the efforts to bring round the workers were still continuing. On hearing this, the Chief Executive, whose office was situated somewhat away from the workspot promptly sent the Industrial Relations Officer. The latter also went round and appealed to the workmen. However, his efforts too did not bear any fruit.

Since there was a recognised Union, with which only parleys could be had, the office bearers were called for negotiations but, they did not turn up. It was noted that they themselves were playing a passive role.

The stalemate continued for three days. While the workmen of every shift were punctually coming and punching their cards, they were not attending to any work and the machines continued to be switched off. The loyal workmen who were willing to resume work were threatened and prevented from doing so. Some workers also indulged in stone throwing, and in immobilising the transport system.

It was not considered proper at that stage to involve the local police as it was likely to precipitate matters and result in sabotage to the plant and machinery worth crores of rupees. The police was however, kept informed.

On a subsequent day, there was commotion all round and the chances of destruction of property were imminent. Therefore, the management decided to impose a lock-out as a sequel to the illegal strike. The management also decided to remove from service a few workmen who were known to be trouble creators by pressing into service the summary powers vested in them as per the standing orders. The management thought that by issuing a notice of intention to lock-out, it could make some of the workmen resume work. Accordingly, it issued the notice of intention to lock-out (Exhibit 1). However prior to this, a further opportunity to resume work was given to the workers through a notice (Exhibit 2).

Immediately after the issue of these notices, a group of men posing themselves as Joint Action Committee (JAC) came forward for negotiations. It may be recalled that, as per the agreement existing between the management and the registered union, the dialogue could be had only with the recognised union and therefore, the union was asked to come forward but they did not turn up. In any case, since the intention of the administration was securing industrial peace and ensuring production, the management allowed them to present a memorandum of grievances and also arranged a meeting between the management and these representatives, whereat, the District Collector, Police officials, Labour Department officials, etc., were also present.

In the course of the meeting as also from the memorandum it came to light that the main cause for the sudden strike was a recruitment where the workmen's children were not given preference. Besides, the workmen had some other demands (Exhibit 3). At the meeting it was explained that the demands could be looked into and that a sudden strike without adhering to the rules, was not justified. It was also made clear that a sizeable number of recruits were relatives of workers, though no such obligation was stipulated by the rules. The representatives, after the discussions, promised to advise the workers to resume work immediately.

Soon after the meeting, some prominent members of the locality came and insisted that the 'locals' should be given preference in jobs since the workshop itself had been constructed on the lands acquired from these 'locals'. It was explained to them that a percentage of recruits were 'locals'. The explanation offered was found satisfactory and they also assured that they would persuade the workers to resume work within two hours.

The representatives of workers as also the prominent members of the locality went round the shops appealing to the workers to resume work. A time was set for the workers to resume work but the workers did not oblige. The workers thought that the management would not resort to lock-out since the administration would be afraid of the ramifications. However, the lock-out did come into effect at 7.10 a.m of the following day from the first shift. Necessary intimations were sent to all concerned in the prescribed forms. A curfew was imposed by the Police in the workshop area. The Police were in full control of the situation. High officials of the State Government were also available at the site. The management had now full time at their disposal to logically arrive at the reasons for the unfortunate development.

As a first step, an official who had earlier worked in that organisation and who was well-known to the workmen and who was not directly connected with the working of the shop was approached to mediate and bring about a settlement. The Officer went round the village where the workers were living and also approached the recognised labour leaders. Surprisingly, it came to light that none knew the real cause of the strike.

On an informal enquiry by some of the officers of the workshop on whom the workmen had tremendous confidence, it came to light that a sizeable number of workers were really interested in resuming work and they never wanted to stop work but did so under pressure and threat. Encouraged by this trend, the trouble creators were identified and dismissed from service. This created a sense of security in the minds of loyal workers and for those workers who were active but not aggressive. This also created in the minds of workers a fear of losing the job. Yet two days passed by with hardly any significant result.

Then, strangely a rumour (which was a surprise even to the management) was afloat that the whole workshop was going to be closed and the plant and machinery was to be shifted to some other place where the organisation had a smaller plant. The rumour aggravated the fear of all the workers and the unrecognised union leaders now thought it fit to come into fray again.

The recognised labour leaders also came forward now. The labour leaders held a meeting away from the place of workshop where there was curfew and the meeting was largely attended. Feelers were sent to the management to lift the lock-out unconditionally.

Messages were spread through the grapevine that the management was never against the workers and that the management was always prepared for lifting the lock-out if the workers were willing to resume work after giving an unconditional written declaration that they would be sincere, honest and would not indulge in vandalism. The declaration was somewhat on the lines of Exhibit 4.

Individual notices were served on the workers informing them of the intention to lift the lock-out and notifying the place where the declaration papers could be signed. The notice was also published in local newspapers (Exhibit 5).

On the appointed day, initially there was a lull till 9 00 a.m. The workers gathered outside in groups. In order to create a sense of safety of workers and to show sincerity of the management, the security force was removed from the site. It was then a sight to see the workers thronging to the place to sign the declaration. Out of 3,000 almost 2,000 signed the declaration in a few hours.

As the response from the workers to sign the declaration was overwhelming, arrangements had to be made for lifting the lock-out and opening the workshop. The *modus operandi* was chalked out after considering the following: (1) from which shift onwards lock-out was to be lifted? (2) what should be the transport arrangement for workers? and (3) how should the workers report? It was also decided that there would be 'no pay for no work'. Then the notice lifting the look-out (Exhibit 6) was issued. Immediately thereafter the workers made a beeline to resume work. They began to work as if nothing had happened.

Exhibit 1: Notice of intention to lock-out

Whereas the workers of ____________________ have illegally struck work from____________________ and inspite of their having been informed through notices and various other methods regarding the illegal stoppage of work and the repercussions thereon, the workers have not resumed work. And whereas this stoppage of work is illegal in terms of Section 24 of the Industrial Disputes Act, 1947 and also in terms of the Essential Services Maintenance Act, 1931, it has therefore been decided to effect a lock-out with effect from __________in accordance with Section 22 of Industrial Disputes Act, 1947. The lock-out shall cover all the workers except the following:

1. Staff of administrative office
2. Supervisors.

The consequences of the lock-out are very serious. The workers and staff are, therefore, requested to resume work immediately and in case not later than_____a.m. on_____. Should this notice go unheeded by the workers and if they continue to refrain from attending to their normal work or adopt any other dilatory tactics or illegal measures, the lock-out, as mentioned above, with all its dire consequences, will come into effect from________a.m. on_____.

Exhibit 2: Strike: Illegal notice thereof

It has come to notice that the staff in________________are not performing their duties. Their concerted action in refusing to work, thereby causing cessation of work and also their failure to adhere to the stipulations laid down under Section 22 of the Industrial Disputed Act, 1947, tantamounts to illegal strike undeı Section 24 of the said Act. The strike being illegal, consequential action as per the Standing Orders automatically comes into force.

Please note that failure to perform the duties and obligations as a servant of the public utility concern will not only result in loss of wages for absence from work but may also constitute a break in service with all attendant consequences besides appropriate disciplinary action.

The striking employees are advised to pause and ponder over the perilous consequences of the illegal strike and desist from continuing the strike, not only in their own interest but in the larger interests of maintaining the essential services for the good of the Public. They are, therefore, advised to go back to duty and perform their work latest by 3.15 p.m. of__________.

Exhibit 3: Charter of Demands

1. The Chief Mechanical Engineer should be transferred.
2. Apprentices given training, should be absorbed at least as 'khalasis' even though Apprentices Act does provide for this.
3. Workload should be fixed.
4. Service Rules should be modified.
5. Ambulance to be maintained in each shop floor.
6. First aid box to be provided.
7. Running of transport should be upto the shop.
8. Canteen facilities and the quaiity of food supplied should be improved.

9. Automatic promotions should be given on completion of six years of service.
10. Transfers, between shops, in the same trade, when asked for, should be agreed to.
11. There should be only two shifts and not three.
12. Victimisation should not be resorted to.
13. Provisions regarding strike clause in the Standing Orders should be cancelled and the consequences of strike should not be imposed on them.
14. Recruitment of khalasis which was done earlier should be cancelled.

Exhibit 4: Undertaking

I,__________son of__________Ticket No.________working as____________in____________shop/section undertakes to adhere strictly to the rules of discipline as per the Standing Orders and *inter alia* comply with all other requirements.

Yours faithfully

Permanent home address (Signature of the employee)

Present home address

Exhibit 5: Notice for lifting the lock-out

Because of the circumstances beyond the control of administration arising out of the illegal strike resorted to by the workmen, lock-out had been declared with effect from first shift of____________________. However, it is understood that the workmen are prepared to withdraw from the illegal strike unconditionally and join duty if the lock-out is lifted. The management is still prepared to lift the lock-out, if majority of the workmen, given an undertaking that they will abide by discipline and will not resort to any go slow, sabotage or any other tactics and join duty and start work without any agitation. Individual undertaking is to be given to the Administration.

For receiving this undertaking, arrangements have been made at__________from________a.m. on________it is reiterated that the issue of this notice does not mean that a decision has been taken to lift the lock-out and the management reserves the right to take this decision after satisfying itself that normal working conditions will prevail.

Exhibit 6: Notice for lifting the lock-out

The lock-out in______________will be lifted temporarily with effect from the shift commencing at 7.10 a.m. on__________. This is being done as a majority of workmen have given an undertaking that they will work in a disciplined and proper manner. Entry into the workshop on______and thereafter till the lifting of lock-out is made final, will be regulated by a permit card which the workers may obtain from ____________________(place and person) after signing the undertaking if they have not already done so.

The transport arrangements are regulated as under:

Route	Timings
________	________
________	________

CASE NO. 10
LATE ATTENDANCE

"Perfect Trading Company" has its office on the first floor of an office-building complex situated in a posh business area in Madras.

Perfect Trading Company has a complement of 70 persons. All the seventy workmen have desk-jobs and have a work schedule of 9.30 a.m. to 4.30 p.m. with a lunch interval between 12.30 p.m. and 1.00 p.m. Attendance in the staff is generally punctual and satisfactory.

The management has laid down a rule, which expects every employee to be at his desk at 9.30 a.m. the opening time of the office. The rule also provides an adjustment of 10 minutes for occasional late attendance due to traffic jams, non-availability of public transport, etc. Another rule specifically mentions that *late attendance on 3 days in a month* would automatically lead to debiting of one day's casual leave. This practice is in vogue for years together in the company.

The rule is being observed generally.

One day Shri Gopalan Nair, an employee of the company, who had earlier reported *late* twice, attended at 9.45 a.m. (i.e. 5 minutes even after the grace period). He was accordingly marked late by 15 minutes and since this was his third time in one month his leave account was debited to the extent of one day's casual leave as per the present rule. This was the normal practice in that office and Office-Manager used to take action suitably. As was the normal routine, the Office Manager sent a note to establishment section, which maintained leave-records of the office staff, instructing to debit one day casual leave against Shri Gopalan Nair's leave account.

Shri Gopalan Nair is an average worker with no bad record. He is a member of the executive of the trade union functioning in the establishment.

The General Secretary, who is also an employee came up with a demand saying that Shri Gopalan Nair was late by five minutes only on the third occasion and, therefore, should not be taken as late on three occasions and one day's casual leave debited to his account should be restored to him.

The management did not agree. Management stated that even on the third occasion he was late by 15 minutes and not five minutes as claimed. The action taken by the management is strictly according to rules and also justified in the context of past practice as well as office discipline.

General Secretary of the 'Perfect Trading Company Employees Union' called a general body meeting on the same evening to protest against the action of the management in debiting one day's leave. He, further, stated in the meeting that Shri Gopalan Nair is an executive member, has a good service record and the management, therefore, should not have taken action against him. Delay of five minutes was hardly anything and definitely not punishable enough to debit one full day. General Secretary wanted all employees to unite and fight against the high-handedness of the management. The employees agreed to follow, strictly, instructions of the Union executive and promised to back them up till last.

On the following day none of the employees entered the establishment. Normally they would walk in and sign the muster and mark the time. By and large, every one would be at his desk before 9.40 a.m. which included grace period of ten minutes granted by the management. The employees, however, formed a queue right from the door till the main road sharp at 9.30 a.m. and started marking time and signing the muster kept near the office door one by one. The process took naturally a long time and by the time the last employee had signed the muster it was already 10.15 a.m.

On enquiry, the management was informed by the General Secretary of the 'Perfect Trading Co. Employees Union' that everybody would attend sharp at 9.30 a.m. but since the office door is too small they could not obviously enter all at one time. Further, each has to mark the time and sign the register and, as such, they have to come in one by one in a proper queue.

The employees marked the time correctly even if it was beyond 9.40 a.m. with a note that they were within the premises of the company even before 9.40 a.m. which was the permissible time, but could not be at their desk, as the small entrance and the muster signing rule won't permit them to rush. They had to, therefore, enter one by one, sign the muster, and fill in the actual correct time of signing the muster, even if it was beyond the permissible time, i.e. 9.40 a.m.

According to the employees the time noted was the time they signed the muster and they claimed that they were present, in fact, all of them on dot at 9.30 a.m. in the office premises of the Perfect Trading Company.

The management overlooked their strange behaviour (which was described by the General Manager as a "childish prank" and 'immature behaviour fit for ignorant crowd') on the first day with the hope that everything would be well on the days to come and they would follow their usual practice of reporting to work, management was grossly disappointed. The employees persisted and it was a strange farce all around the area and particularly in that building, which was a big office complex and accommodated many known business houses. The situation, obviously, was very embarrassing to the Perfect Trading Company.

It must be said to the credit of the employees that there was no demonstration, no slogan-shouting, and but for their queuing up and marching one by one in the office for signing the muster in the morning, the work went on well, in fact even better, once they reached their allotted Table. The 'single-file march' was so well-organised by the union, that out of the seventy employees at least ten to fifteen would sign the register after 9.40 a.m. everyday.

The General Manager who had generally good relations with the General Secretary of the Union tried to find out as to what the union actually wants and what would bring back normally in working of the company. Through a common friend the management was informed that the Union desires that Shri Gopalan Nair should not be marked late, as done by the management and that his one day casual leave debited should be restored to him.

Management of Perfect Trading Company was also informed by a letter, that Shri Gopalan Nair was unanimously elected Assistant Secretary of the Perfect Trading Company Employees Union in the last meeting in place of Shri Kailasa who had resigned from the executive body of the union.

Questions

1. (a) Give a critical analysis of the case, with special reference to the behaviour of the employees about a rule which was in vogue for years together.
   (b) Could this be treated as 'Ignorant crowd behaviour' or 'Childish prank' as termed by the General Manager?
2. (a) Would you recommend disciplinary action and if so what would be the charge?
   (b) Can the 'behaviour' pattern of the employees constitute 'Misconduct' as understood in industrial relations?

3. (a) What steps would you take in the situation?
   (b) Would it be right for the management to mark late against those who have been signing the muster roll after 9.40 a.m. though they were in the premises of the office much before 9.40 a.m.?
   (c) Can you suggest some alternative?
   (d) Is there any special significance to Shri Gopalan Nair being an executive committee member earlier and his then becoming Assistant Secretary of the Perfect Trading Company Employees' Union?
4. Would you like to issue a small 'hand-out' to the Press in support of your case? If so how would you word it?
5. Would you agree to the demand of the Union in view of the embarrassing situation created for the company in that area of well-known business houses, by the behaviour of the employees?

First Alternative Answer

1. This behaviour of the employees cannot be treated as 'ignorant crowd behaviour' 'childish prank' as termed by the General Manager. The behaviour of the employees is a well planned and organised action to show their dissatisfaction for the action taken by the G.M. on Shri Gopalan Nair. 'Childish prank' means mischievous behaviour of children but the behaviour of the employees is not like that. It is a planned, purposeful and premeditated behaviour. They go by the rules of the Perfect Trading Company.
2. I would not recommend disciplinary action against the workers. They are guided by their Trade Union.
   (a) No. The behaviour pattern of the employees does not constitute 'Misconduct'.
3. In the above situation, I would, first consult the Trade Union. I would try to find out a consensus in this matter.
   (b) It is not a right action for the management to mark late against those who have been signing the

muster roll after 9.40 a.m. Because they were in the premises of the office much before 9.40 a.m.

(c) My suggestion is as follows: The management should construct a new wide entrance so that forming of queue can be avoided. The workers may be asked to go to their respective seats. An attendant may be asked to get the signature of the employees in the register. Or the management should have department-wise register instead of one common register for all.

(d) Yes, there is a special significance to Shri Gopalan Nair being an executive committee member earlier and he, then, becoming Assistant Secretary of the Perfect Trading Company Employees' Union.

4. No, I would not like to issue a 'hand-out' to the press.
5. Yes, I would agree to the demand of the Union.

Second Alternative Answer

1. Perfect Trading Company has seventy workmen. They have a work schedule of 9.30 a.m. to 4.30 p.m. with a lunch interval between 12.30 p.m. and 1.00 p.m. Attendance in the staff is generally punctual. The rule of the management allows 10 minutes late attendance on two days in a month. Late attendance on three days in a month would automatically lead to debiting of one day's casual leave. The rule is followed by all. Shri Gopal Nair came late third time in one month. As per the rule, it was treated as one day's casual leave.

   (b) The behaviour of the employees could be treated as 'ignorant crowd behaviour' or 'Childish prank'.

2. Yes, I would recommend disciplinary action, under Sections 2(g) and 3(2) of Industrial Employment (Standing Order) Act, 1946.

   (b) Yes, the behaviour pattern of the employees constitute 'Misconduct'.

3. I would take suitable actions to prevent this behaviour pattern of the employees.

(b) Yes, it is right on the part of the management to mark late against those who have been signing the muster roll after 9.40 a.m.

(c) The employees were in the premises of the office much before 9.40 a.m. The door of the office would be altered to facilitate all to enter at one time. The process which accounted for delay in signing the muster would be changed by opening section-wise attendance register.

(d) Yes, there is a special significance to Shri Gopalan Nair becoming Assistant Secretary of the Perfect Trading Company Employees' Union.

4. I would like to issue the following 'hand-out' to the press in support of my case:

PERFECT TRADING COMPANY

Violation of Standing Order Rule

Attendance in the staff was punctual for years together in our company. The rule relating to late coming was being observed generally by all. Is it justifiable for the employees to support Gopalan Nair who violated the rule relating to attendance and late coming which is in vogue from the inspection of the company till date? A time to think and support the management stand.

General Manager, Perfect Trading Company

5. I would not agree to the demand of the Union.

CASE NO. 11
WORK STOPPAGE

Sri Chandi Metal Works Ltd. is an undertaking of the Government of India and produces some special qualities of steel and certain steel products. It has a workforce of around 7,000 employees. There are four unions, each of them affiliated to separate national trade union centres. Among them, Sri Chandi Employees Union (SCEU) is recognized by the management as the sole 'bargaining' agent. It commands majority support of workers in the entire organisation taken together, but in some of the individual departments other unions have greater strength. For example, in the Research and Chemicals Laboratory of the Company another union known as Sri Chandi Metal Workers' Union (SCMWU) has a membership of about 95 per cent of the employees. SCMWU has also considerable following in some other departments and commands majority support in the Forge Shop also. The other two unions are relatively less significant, but they have some followers in almost every department and one of them, viz., Sri Chandi Labour Union (SCLU) dominates in the central office of the organisation.

In early 1978, there was considerable commotion in the R and C Laboratory of the organisation on the issue of the promotion policy in general and some specific cases of promotions in particular. These promotions were granted to certain employees of R and C Laboratory on the basis of common seniority as represented by the length of service in Sri Chandi Metal Works as a whole, as against the length of service in specific grades of R and C Laboratory. As a result of the acceptance of this principle of common seniority in the organisation, it was alleged that only the members of the recognised union (SCEU) gained, as all the promoted persons belonged to that union. The other rival unions and particularly SCMWU, which had a commanding strength in R and C Laboratory and the Forge shop, took serious objection to it and started an agitation on the ground that in future all promotions must be only on the basis of seniority in the particular two or three grades immediately below the grades having vacancies to be filled through promotion. To this, SCEU took strong exception and they started a counter-agitation insisting on the formal acceptance of the common seniority in the organisation as the main basis of promotions. Although the management did not take a formal policy decision on this matter, SCMWU and two other non-recognized unions alleged that some of the top officers of the organisation, including the Chief Metallurgist Mr. N. Dar, and the General Superintendent, Mr. Mansur Ali, were partial to SCEU and were adopting the common seniority principle in effect in all cases of promotion mainly as a result of their partial attitude. In their discussion with the representatives of these unions and others, these two officers, however, strongly denied this allegation. As against this, the recognized union alleged that the Chief Chemist of R and C Laboratory, Mr. S. Pal, was backing the rival unions and particularly SCMWU for his own narrow ends. Naturally Mr. Pal also strongly denied this allegation.

The inter-union, rivalry in the R and C Laboratory became entangled with another unusual issue at this time. The relation between the Chief Chemist, Mr. Pal and the General Foreman of R and C Laboratory, Mr. S. Chakraborty, was not happy. Earlier they belonged to the same-rank and in 1977, Mr. Pal was promoted over Mr. Chakraborty as the Chief Chemist, when the post fell vacant due to retirement of the earlier incumbent to it. On many occasions Mr. Chakraborty criticized the official decisions of Mr. Pal and one day they had a physical clash in front of their subordinates. The hidden rivalry then came into the open and in this, the workers of the section were also involved. The employees belonging to SCMWU and SCLU supported Mr. Pal and those belonging to SCFU supported Mr. Chakraborty.

Thus, on various issues the relations between the unions and the management, between different union themselves and among different officers were somewhat strained in Sri Chandi Metal Works, although there was no major eruption of such strains into open frictions till June 1978.

In June 1978, however, there was an unexpected development in the factory which had broken this apparent peace on the surface and the operations came to a standstill. It happened on a very minor issue of job-rotation in the R and C Laboratory. About a year back, there was a dacoity in a nearby village in which Mr. L.N. Das, a duty-cum-leave reserve sampler of the R and C Laboratory, resided. He made an appeal to the Chief Chemist of the R and C Laboratory, who was the officer in-charge of the sampling section, for changing his shift-cycle so that he might attend duty in the day-shift every day and could return home with other workers of Sri Chandi Metal Works coming from the same village. The Chief Chemist considered the appeal sympathetically and requested another duty-cum-leave reserve sampler. Mr. N. Gorai, who at that time was working in the day shift to interchange his duty-cycle with Mr. L.N. Das. Mr. Gorai initially did not agree to this change, but on further persuasion accepted the proposed change of shift. However, according to him and the representatives of SCMEU, of which he was a member, he agreed to the change only on a temporary basis and did not signify his formal consent to the proposed change by signing the official form of application for the shift-change, although that was the usual procedure.

After a few months work according to the new shift-cycle, Mr. Gorai requested the authorities to send him back to his earlier shift-cycle. As there was no response, he presented a formal application for the same in May 1978, asking for an interchange of his cycle with Mr. L.N. Das maintaining that the arrangement of the change in shift-cycles had been temporary. This, however, was not acceptable to the latter, who had the backing of SCMWU in this stand. The recognized Union SCMEU, therefore, decided to come forward to support its member, viz., Mr. Gorai. The matter, thus, turned into an issue of inter-union rivalry and prestige.

With the situation becoming very difficult, the matter was referred to the Chief Chemist, who initially tried to settle it by having discussions with the particular individuals and unions concerned. But no agreed solution could be reached. He, then, issued instructions for a new shift-cycle for all the duty-cum-leave reserve samplers. In protest the samplers belonging to the three non-recognized unions stopped work the next day. On the intervention of the Senior Personnel Officer, the work was resumed on the assurance that the whole matter would be considered again before the new shift-cycle was given effect. The Chief Metallurgist of the organisation then intervened and held discussions with top leaders of various unions, but still no settlement could be reached. About 5 days afterwards on the 18th June, the Chief Chemist, under the instructions of his superior (i.e., the Chief Metallurgist), issued new orders interchanging the shifts of only Mr. Das, and Mr. Gorai, without affecting other duty-cum-leave reserve samplers. The new shift-cycles was to be effective from the 20th June 1978.

On June 20, Mr. Das, who was assigned duty in the second shift on the new shift-cycle, came for duty in the morning shift. The shift-in-charge did not give him attendance for this shift. In protest, the regular samplers of the shift refused to work. They also did not allow Mr. Gorai and other willing workers belonging to SCMEU to work. As a result, the samples sent from the Steel Melting Shop (SMS) could not be analyzed. The officers of R and C Laboratory, steel melting shop, and the personnel department then jointly tried to persuade the striking workers to resume work. But they did not succeed. Meanwhile, the workers belonging to SCMEU gathered in strength and demanded that the management should make arrangements so that the willing workers could work on the samples and the works of other departments were unaffected. But all negotiations failed to end the work stoppage in the sampling section of the R and C Laboratory. After waiting for some more time, the superintendent of S.M.S., issued instructions to switch off the furnaces there, as it was dangerous to keep hot liquid metals in them for an indefinite period and because no further work in his shop was possible without getting the analysis of the samples sent from the sampling section.

Prolonged negotiations between the management, and different unions continued through the whole day on the 20th and also in the morning and afternoon of the 21st. Around 4 p.m. the two groups of workers almost tended to clash and it appeared that the situation would go out of control. The police arrived, but at the request of the union leaders and with the consent of the management they left the spot, as leaders of different unions started negotiations among themselves. Ultimately a solution was reached among the unions. This was communicated to the management and they accepted it. According to this settlement, the instructions issued by the Chief Chemist on the 18th June were cancelled and the *status quo* regarding the shift-duties of Mr. Das and Mr. Gorai was maintained till the 27th June. With effect from the 28th, a new shift-cycle would be introduced with provision that Mr. Das and Mr. Gorai would change their shifts every three months. It was further agreed that the management in consultation with the unions would work out a new scheme outlining the basis of the rotation of duties of samplers. Till the finalisation of that scheme the arrangement under the settlement made on the 21st June, 1978, would continue. A formal Agreement containing the terms of this settlement was signed by the representatives of the management and the four Unions concerned. After that the normal operations in R and C Laboratory and S.M.S. were resumed from 5.30 p.m. on the 21st June, 1978.

Questions

1. What according to you were the apparent and fundamental reasons behind the work stoppage in R and C Laboratory and S.M.S. of Sri Chandi Metal Works?
2. For prevention of repetition of similar troubles in these two departments, or in others, what are the steps which the management may take?
3. Comment on the ways the management handled the situation. What else could they do under the given circumstances?

Answers:

1. The fundamental reasons behind a work stoppage are:

   (a) There is Inter-Union rivalry. (b) Common seniority principle is opposed by the SCMWU. (c) The management does not have a formal policy decision regarding promotion. (d) The Chief Chemist of R and C Laboratory, Mr. S. Pal is supporting the SCMWU for his own narrow ends. The relation between the chief chemist, Mr. Pal and the General Foreman of R and C Laboratory, Mr. S. Chakraborty, was not cordial. Earlier they belonged to the same rank and in 1977, Mr. Pal was promoted over Mr. Chakraborty as the Chief Chemist. Mr. Chakraborty criticized the official decision. He struck Mr. Pal with his fist in the presence of their subordinates. The workers belonging to SCMWU and SCLU supported Mr. Pal and those belonging to SCFU supported Mr. Chakraborty. (e) The next reason is the issue of job-rotation (shift-cycle).

2. The management should revise its policies relating to promotion, and job-rotation. Seniority-cum-merit should be the basis for promotion. Workers' education is needed. The workers and the supervisors must be imparted basic knowledge relating to personnel management and inter-personnel relationship must be developed. 'One union one industry' concept will be the solution to prevent inter-union rivalry. For that there is need for making of unions into one single union. There should be no room for whims and fancies in the implementation of rules and regulations. Efficient and experienced men should be posted as supervisors. Strict discipline is to be enforced. Co-ordination and involvement of all workers help to achieve the objectives of the management.
3. The management of Sri Chandi Metal Works Ltd. had failed to create a smooth relation with the workers. It had created a hostile work atmosphere. The management did not set right the fragile matters such as promotion and job-rotation. The management did not act in a shrewd manner while dealing with a delicate situation but in an immature way that not only affected the work in the sampling section but in the S.M.S. The supervisor interchanged the shift-cycles without getting the formal consent of both the employees while signing the official form of application for the shift change. He deviated from the usual procedure. Mr. Gorai appealed to the authorities to change his shift but there was no response for his request.

The Chief Chemist intervened only after the situation became grave and he further more worsened the matter by changing the shift of all the workers. An individual's problem developed into a group dispute and he made all the workers hostile to the management leading to work stoppage. Even the chief metallurgist failed to handle the situation wisely. He did not encourage upward communication. The supervisors are the pillars of the organisation but they were not taught how to develop smooth relations with the workers. The grievance of Mr. Das was not redressed properly. The management in this case was always taking the reactive measures but failed to take the proactive measures.

The management could have created a sense of belongingness among the workers. What the management had done at the end could have been possible at the beginning because the union leaders were also not for work stoppage.

CASE NO. 12
DEMAND OF THE UNION

Raju was an apprentice trainee in a large public sector project. While on job during the training period he was involved in a fatal accident. He was not a member of the Union. Still the Union took up his case and asked for funeral advance. When the management was hesitant to take an immediate decision, the Union threatened the management with wild cat strike. The management paid the advance. Two days later the Union insisted that the management must pay compensation as per Workmen's Compensation Act. The management maintained that at the time of his death Raju was not an employee and so he was not eligible for compensation. The management was afraid that it would set a bad precedent. The compensation works out to Rs. 20,000. The Union maintained that it costs less than the cost of one dinner that the management hosts whenever a VIP visits the project. In the absence of a favourable response from the management, the union want on strike.

Questions

1. What are the issues? Is the demand of the union justified?

Answer

The issues are the following:

(i) One Mr. Raju, an apprentice trainee in a public sector project, met with fatal accident while on job.

(ii) The union demanded compensation as per Workmen's Compensation Act.

(iii) Whether Raju is eligible for compensation?

(iv) Is the strike of the Union legal or illegal?

The demand of the union is justified on humanitarian ground. Though Mr. Raju is an apprentice, his loss of life has brought out untold sorrow and misery to the bereaved family.

2. Evaluate the response of the management

Solution A

The response of the management to the demand of the union is not justifiable. The management failed to visualise and realise the trauma and financial hardship faced by the bereaved family of Mr. Raju. The initial hesitant of the management in giving funeral advance to the bereaved family is highly condemnable. The contention of the management that Mr. Raju was not an employee at the time of death is highly deplorable.

3. Suggest how the problem should be tackled at this stage

Answer

The management can give employment to any one of the members of Raju's family.

Solution B: For Question No. 1

Does the Workmen's Compensation Act, 1923 (and its Amendment in 1984) cover the apprentice? When is accident compensation payable? How much can be given as compensation for death? Whether the Union's strike is legal and justifiable? These are the issues of the given case.

In this connection, it may be mentioned that as it is customary with every Labour law, controversies have arisen over the question of the interpretation of the word 'workman' as defined in the Act. The court's concerned in trailing the cases have held many other categories of persons as workmen. In this way, according to a ruling of the High Court of Madras, piece-rated workers, apprentices and honorary workers should also be deemed as covered by the Act (K.V.V. Sharma *Vs.* State 1953 I LLU 29).

The employer of any establishment covered under this Act, is required to compensate an employee:

(a) who has suffered an accident arising out of and in the course of his employment, resulting into:
  (i) death,
  (ii) permanent total disablement,
  (iii) permanent partial disablement, or
  (iv) temporary disablement whether total or partial.

(b) who has contracted an occupational diseases.

Extent of the injury	*Quantum*
Where death results from the injury:	An amount equal to 40 per cent of the monthly wages of the deceased workman multiplied by the relevant factor specified in Sch. IV, or An amount of Rs. 20,000 whichever is more.

Hence, the demand of the union is justified.

Answer Q. No. 2 (i) Chapter III of Trade Unions Act, 1926 deals with rights and liabilities of registered trade unions. Chapter V of Industrial Disputes Act, 1947 deals with strikes and lock-outs. The demand of the union in this case is a genuine demand. In the given case, the union threatened the management with wild cat strike. 'Wild cat strike' means unofficial and irresponsible strike by workers. Of course, no person employed in a public utility service shall go on strike in breach of contract:

(a) without giving to the employer notice of strike, as hereinafter provided, within six weeks before striking; or

(b) within 14 days of giving such notice; or

(c) before the expiry of the date of strike specified in any such notice as aforesaid; or

(d) during the pendency of any conciliation proceedings before a conciliation officer and 7 days after the conclusion of such proceedings.

A strike shall be illegal if it is commenced or declared in contravention of Section 22 or 23 (Chapter V) of Industrial Disputes Act, 1947.

Suggestion: Through negotiation, the problem can be solved. Failing which the legal remedy can be taken. The management should follow ethics of business.

CASE NO. 13
LOCOMOTIVE DRIVERS

Ramesh Works Ltd., was a heavy engineering unit established in 1929. It was a railway haulage industrial unit. The company is engaged in the haulage and transfer of steel and other materials including finished goods from one department to another department and from one railway station to another railway station. It had eight steam locomotives. They were purchased twenty-eight years before. They faced many repair and maintenance problems. Therefore, the company decided to replace them by six new diesel locomotives. While taking this decision, they studied the comparative advantage of the steam and diesel locomotives. Diesel locomotive is quicker. It has better haulage and it needs only 15 minutes for fuelling once a day; whereas the steam locomotives spent about four hours to take coal and water. Diesel locomotive can easily be switched off and are economical to operate.

As soon as the first locomotive was received, the management decided to train the diesel drivers. Many of them were uneducated. There was a two-month training programme and the company decided to relieve the steam drivers from their work. Steam locomotive was manned by a driver and a fire-man. But for diesel locomotives, there was no need for fire-man. Moreover, there was no enough space in the driving place for a second man. Hence, the management decided to absorb the surplus fire-men in other vacancies without any loss in their earnings. A spare driver was provided for every three locomotives to relieve each regular driver for two hours.

The recognised trade union was kept informed about the changes and the union raised no objection at that time. However, when the new diesel locomotives were commissioned with a driver each to man them, the loco crew opposed, made a complaint to the trade union and sent a strong protest-note to the General Manager and wanted the matter to be discussed in detail before any change was introduced. The secretary of the Trade Union pointed out in his letter that the drivers would not be able to drive the diesel locomotives for six hours without assistants to help them and it would also block the promotion opportunity of fire-men who were rendered surplus. Two men in each locomotive would have a better view of both sides of the track which was necessary for safe driving. The trade union insisted on spare drivers to relieve regular drivers having long hours of work. The management finally agreed to discuss the issue with the union before implementing them.

Questions

1. What should have been done to avoid this situation?

Answer: Replacement of the steam locomotives by diesel locomotives is a very good step. It has a lot of advantage over steam locomotives. Diesel locomotive does not require two crew members. It is a wastage of manpower. In each and every organisation there will be organisational change and development. The management ought to have cleared the psychological fear of retrenchment and lay-off. among the workers by persuasion and personnel counselling. The management should agree to observe the surplus fire-men in other vacancies without any loss in their earnings. Traing programme may be conducted to fit in the fire-men in other jobs. The management ought to have consulted and convinced the trade union before implementing any new proposal.

2. Is it right on the part of the union to make a demand for two crew members to diesel locomotive? Substantiate your answer.

Answer: I think it is not right on the part of the union to make a demand for two crew members for one diesel locomotive. Because, diesel locomotive does not require coal and hence, there is no question of taking care of burning coal. Moreover, there is no chance of flying of ash. Since the space available in the driving-room is small, there is no need for a second man to help the driver.

3. ***Is it correct on the part of the management to have agreed to discuss the issues with union?***

Answer: Agreeing to discuss the issues with the union is correct. Workers' participation in management is an accepted concept. Nothing wrong in consulting the union before formulating a new policy and after implementing the agreed new policy.

4. What stand the management should take in the discussion?

Answer: The management should be stubborn in introducing diesel locomotives. The fire-men may be transferred to some other department/sections. Vountary Retirement Scheme (VRS) may introduced and willing surplus workers may be allowed to avail the scheme. Periodical meeting with trade union leaders and workers may be conducted by the management and thereby active involvement of workers in the modernisation programme can be achieved. Of course, 'give and take policy' is the best policy for any organisational development.

5. Learning value of this case

Organisational resistance will be there for any organisational change. Orientation, persuasion, consultation, discussion and concurrence for any new decision is a must. Psychological stress and fear among the workers have to be eradicated by the management. Career development, training programme and empowerment of workers are the areas of consideration and concentration for the progress and prosperity of an organisation.

CASE NO. 14
"KHAN DIDN'T MAKE IT"

Heavy Instruments Ltd., was a large undertaking employing a manpower of 50,000. The main production unit consisted of several large departments in operations and maintenance. The company had eleven layers in the non-executive level.

Vacancies were filled up through one of the following methods:

(a) Direct recruitment from the open market.

(b) Promotion of eligible employees as per lines of promotion through the departmental promotion committee.

(c) Internal circulars confined to the employees working in particular department or alternatively through internal circulars open to all the employees of the unit as per the conditions of eligibility.

If there was a vacancy in a grade, a departmental promotion committee was constituted for promoting the eligible person from the next lower grade in the same line in promotion. The committee consisted of the departmental head and an officer from the Personnel Department. The minimum eligibility period for promotion from one grade to another was three years.

If there was an urgent need to fill up a vacancy and the persons in the next lower grade were not eligible for promotion due to non-fulfilment of the minimum eligibility period or otherwise, internal circular were issued inviting applications from the persons belonging to the same department.

If even the eligible persons were not found, the coverage of the internal circular was extended to all the departments of the unit for filling up the vacancy.

For promotion, seniority-cum-merit was the criteria. In the case of internal circulars, however, merit was the only criteria for selection. In the case of a tie, the senior-most candidate was selected.

In one of the maintenance departments at one time there were four vacancies for the post of Crane operators in Grade I. There were many operators in the lower grade, i.e. Grade II but none of them had completed the minimum eligibility period. The head of the department felt that these vacancies should be filled up urgently and recommended that an internal circular be issued.

Then the Personnel Department issued an internal circular in March 2008 inviting applications from candidates who had completed two years in the Grade II level within that department. As per the policy, the selection was to be done through a two-stage screening process consisting of technical efficiency test and interview. The technical efficiency test was conducted by a committee consisting of representatives from the concerned department, Training Department and Personnel Department.

In the present case, the operators were required to operate the same equipment which they were operating in Grade II because even after their selection and absorption as Grade I operators they would be required to operate the same equipment.

Five applications were received. The senior-most among the five was Khan whose past performance was satisfactory. Satisfactory rating was given to such persons whose performance was just tolerable; it did not debar them from promotion. The interview and the technical efficiency test was conducted in May 2008. Khan failed in the test, and the junior-most person among the five topped the list.

For various reasons, the list of the selected candidates was not officially notified for three months. In the middle of July the five operators stopped work and obstructed the work of others for 16 hours in protest against the delay.

Then, the selection order of the four candidates was notified and Khan's name did not figure in that. Khan intervened saying that he was dropped because he belonged to a particular union and the other four were selected because all of them belonged to another union. Khan's union also backed him and insisted that selection was biased. The industrial relations situation in the department gradually started deteriorating.

Questions

1. ***Discuss the key issues. Explain how the matter could have been handled?***

Heavy Instrument Ltd., is a big concern where 50,000 employees are employed. The company has 11 layers in the non-executive level. Vacancies are filled by direct recruitment, by internal circulars and by promotion. The minimum eligibility condition for promotion is three years' experience in the given cadre. Candidates are selected on merit-cum-seniority basis. There are four vacancies for the post of Crane operator at grade one level. Five applications are received for this post. Khan is one among them. He is the senior-most person. His performance in his department is also good but he failed in the technical test. He is a member of a particular union. Except Khan, three other persons are promoted by the management. He makes a protest against this. The Trade Union also supports him. This is the key issue in this case. This matter could have been handled by sending internal circular methods and convening meeting and arriving at a consensus in the selection process and methods.

2. *At this stage of the probe, what kind of options does the management have to deal with it? What steps should management initiate?*

There are the following options for the management to deal with the above stated problems:

(i) Out of four vacancies, two might have been filled up by following direct recruitment method and remaining one by promotion and another by internal circular confined to the employees working in particular department.

(ii) Alternatively all the four vacancies may be filled up through internal circulars open to all the employees of the unit as per the conditions of eligibility.

(iii) One person may be selected by merit basis, another person on seniority basis and remaining two from the open market by direct recruitment method.

CASE NO. 15
IMPACT OF OLD AGE

Tikka Re-rolling Mills is a company where 3,000 employees are employed in its various units. In these units, steel billets trough square bars (50-125 sqmm) obtained from steel plants were heated to 1300 degree centigrade in reheating furnace and were rolled into smaller sections according to the requirements of the market. This process involves many stages. It was controlled by three operators who worked on a raised platform called 'the rolling gallery' just by the side of the mill. The work demanded quick reflex action as well as effective co-ordination among the three operators.

Mr. Ramesh, aged 56, a senior operative is one among the three operators forming a group to work on 'the rolling gallery'. He joined the company as a semi-skilled worker at the age of 21 and has risen to his present position by clink of hard work. Now, he became ineffective and the production of the number of billets dropped. His supervisors thought that it was due to his advancing age, because his colleagues are 35 years and 40 years old. As the situation became worse, the department manager recommended the General Manager to replace Mr. Ramesh by a younger operator. But the General Manager was not ready to do the same because 35 per cent of the company's employees were over 50 years old and others might be greatly perturbed, feeling that it might happen to any of them. The general feeling among the workers was also the same and the recognized workers' union was also in sympathy with Mr. Ramesh and were against his replacement. Thus, the matter came up for consideration at a meeting of senior executive presided over by the General Manager.

In the meeting, the General Manager expressed the view that replacement of Mr. Ramesh due to his old age might not be the best way of handling the situation; if so the other department managers might request the same and the union would also agree to such a proposal. Since the normal retirement age of the employees was 60 and since about one-third of the employees are over 50 years, it is impossible to replace Mr. Ramesh.

The Personnel Officer expressed his views that if the old operators are rehabilitated in other departments of lighter jobs, it may block the promotion opportunities of men in those departments and they may face some other adjustment and job accommodation problems.

At the end of the meeting, the importance of formulation of a definite policy to deal with the present problem and of the future problems of the same situation was felt. But how?

Questions

1. What are the problems involved in this case?

Answer: Here, the problematic situation arises due to the old age of an employee, i.e. the impact of an old age. This is not the problem of an individual but it will be the problem for employees. Due to aging effect and inefficiency, the production of the company decreases. Mr. Ramesh became ineffective because of his old age. To find a way out, the departmental manager recommended for his replacement to the General Manager. Here comes (i) the problem of replacement, (ii) problem of rehabilitation and (iii) the formulation of a definite policy to overcome these problems in the future.

2. Suggest the solution to avoid such a situation.

Answer: As the problem directly hits the production of the company, it has to be solved quickly and prudently. It must be solved once for all and should not be allowed to repeat. Hence, the following solutions are suggested:

Solution No. 1: Exchange of work/Job rotation

The work of Mr. Ramesh involves three operatives who worked on the raised platform quickly with co-ordinative action. Since the work involves three different actions from three operatives, the lighter operative work(action) may be given to the old aged employee Mr. Ramesh.

Solution No. 2: Formulating promotion policy

The promotion policy must be framed in such a way that the semi-skilled workers after joining the work must, with their hard work and experience, attain a supervisory position which does not involve much physical effort, (or)

Promotion may be given on seniority-cum-merit basis. The promoted employees must be given training and orientation to fit the new work given to them. Some other rehabilitation scheme may be introduced and lighter jobs in other departments may be assigned.

Question 3: What is the legal aspect of the given case.

Answer: The standing order may be altered and the age of retirement may be reduced legally. Physically inefficient and aged workers may be directed to avail VRS or compulsory retirement may be introduced to such employees.

CASE NO. 16
A CASE OF DISMISSAL

Industrial Employment Standing Order of the company "X" provides that an Enquiry Officer for enquiring into any misconduct under Certified Standing Order has to be an officer nominated by the company. However, for the past so many years, it was the practice of the company to appoint outsiders as enquiry officer for conducting enquiry into any misconduct under Standing Order. The past enquiries were never objected either by the union or by any charge-sheeted employee.

Recently, in one case, on the basis of the findings of the enquiry, the management served a show cause notice to an employee as to why he should not be dismissed from service for the omission and commission done by him. The charge-sheeted employee participated throughout the enquiry. Later, he challenged the show cause notice issued by the management on the ground that the enquiry is *void ab initio* as the enquiry could be conducted only by an officer nominated by the company and not by an outsider. He supported his points with two authoritative judgments—one High Court and another Supreme Court. The Honourable Courts are of the opinion that if the Standing Order prescribes that an enquiry has to be conducted by an officer nominated by the company, any enquiry by an outsider is not tenable in the eyes of law. The company's legal counsel is also of the opinion that according to the provisions of the Standing Order, the enquiry officer must be an officer of the company and no outsider can be appointed for the purpose. The management is, now, in a dilemma as to what to do.

Questions

1. ***Whether the management should go ahead with the dismissal and face the legal battle in the courts?***

Answer: No, the management should not go ahead with the dismissal. The management has to be advised not to proceed further in this legal battle. Because, the charge sheeted employee has challenged the show cause notice of the management on the ground that the enquiry is void.

2. ***Whether the management should condone this case and should conduct a fresh enquiry by an officer of the company instead of appointing an outsider?***

Answer: The management should reduce the punishment from dismissal to suspension and conduct a fresh enquiry by appointing an officer in the company itself.

3. ***Is there any need for modifying the standing order?***

Yes. With the approval of the certifying officer, the management should discuss with the union to modify the standing order and find an amicable solution to solve the problem not only in the present case but also in the future.

4. ***What is the legal validity of enquiry already concluded and based on which the actions taken by the management?***

Answer: The enquiry already concluded and action taken based on the enquiry is null and void. To make provision for conducting enquiry by an outsider, the standing order should be modified with the consent of the certifying officer and trade union. If the fresh enquiry endorses the previous conclusion, then the action taken by the management is legally valid.

CASE NO. 17
ARRESTING THE NEIGHBOUR'S KID

Barney Kohl is a Police Officer assigned to the juvenile department of a large city. Part of the oath that Barney took was to uphold the law consistently for all people. The scope of his job includes investigation of youth drug traffic, alcoholism and vandalism. Barney is also involved in the community outreach programme, which works to build greater understanding and cooperation between the Police Department and the youth of the community.

Last night, Barney ran into one of the most difficult, if not the most dangerous, problems he has ever faced. While on patrol, he received a radio report to investigate some possible vandalism at a junior high school. Upon reaching the scene he found five youths, aged 12 to 15, engaged in malicious acts of vandalism. They were throwing rocks through the windows and had splashed paint on the walls. After calling backup units, he proceeded to run down and arrested the vandals. He was successfully holding the group at bay and was waiting for the backup unit to arrive when he noticed that one of the offenders was his neighbour's son. The city has a parent's responsibility law that makes parent's financially liable for the damage caused by their children's actions. The damaged looked as if it would be considerable, probably running into thousands of dollars. Barney knows that his neighbour cannot afford the costs. He is crippled and out of work. He also knows that this incident will lead to great problems in their family and, of course, would place a great strain on his own and his family's relationship with the neighbours.

Questions

1. *What kind of conflict is this police officer experiencing? What should he do?*

Answer: Conflict is that it is any tension which is experienced when one person perceives that one's needs or desires are likely to be thwarted or frustrated. According to Follett, it is the appearance of difference of opinions, and of interest. The type of conflict experienced by the Police Officer is intra-personal conflict. Intra-individual conflict occurs within himself. His role as a police officer clashes with his affection towards his neighbour's son. As a sincere officer he should be duty conscious and should not be influenced by emotion or tension or relation with his neighbour. He must act according to the eyes of law.

2. How do you explain the boy's behaviour in terms of the frustration model?

Youth aged 12 to 15 in a Junior High School indulged in drug traffic, alcoholism and vandalism. When Barney Kohl, a police officer, received a radio report to investigate this and when he reached the school, he found 5 boys engaged in malicious acts of vandalism. The balked boys frustrated and started throwing stones and damaging walls. Frustration occurs when a motivated drive is blocked before a person reaches a desired goal. The goal here may be exchanging intoxicated drink or selling/exchanging drugs. There is aggression and violence in the school campus. It is the duty of the police officer to eliminate the frustrating barriers out of people's way.

3. If you were asked to conduct a training seminar for police officers on the management of conflict, what topics would you cover? What strategies would you suggest?

I would cover the topics like 'conflict due to frustration', 'goal conflict', 'role conflict and ambiguity', 'interactive conflict', 'interpersonal conflict', 'inter-group behaviour and conflict', 'intra-individual conflict', etc., I would suggest the following strategies:

(i) Behavioural self-control,

(ii) Cognitive therapy,

(iii) Relaxation,

(iv) Exercise, Negotiation skills etc.,

Preventive measures, and Curative measures may be dealt with in the seminar.

CASE NO: 18
CASUAL SHOE

The shoe market in India can be divided into two major segments, namely the formal leather shoes and the casual wear shoes. There has been a rapid change in the causal shoes market in the past few years in India. It is no more a distinctive possession of the elite only. It has now become a ubiquitous, all purpose shoe as the outlook of people towards casual shoes has also changed. The market is now set for a boom. This is also owing to the launch of many new range of casual shoes by Bata and Carona in technical collaboration with the world famous leading manufacturers of shoes like Adidas and Puma respectively. In a study of casual shoes, we found that top of the mind awareness for various brands were North Star (33%), Nike (38%), Puma (14%) and Adidas (15%). Although Bata and Carona have been existing in the market for a long time, there has been scores of new entrants such as Liberty, Dawood, etc., and even some foreign brands. This has led to an increased competition. It would be worthwhile to do an exploratory study of the casual shoe market with the aim of understanding consumer behaviour, buying criterion, awareness and preference of brands, attitudes of consumers, etc.

Research Objectives

1. Understanding consumer behaviour

- Particularly to analyse the type of buying behaviour—whether it is value for money, variety seeking, dissonance reducing or habitual pattern noticed in casual shoe selection.

2. Criterion used and their importance in the purchase decision

- Specially ascertain how style, durability, price, comfort, status, etc., attributes play a decisive role in the consumers decision-making process.

3. Awareness of brand name and reference

- What are the brands that consumers are aware (i.e., unaided recall)?
- What is the level of awareness of brands like Power, North Star, Puma, Nike, Adidas, Dawood, Liberty and some foreign brands of casual shoes?
  - Do the consumers show any distinct preference for any set of brands?
  - Do the consumers feel some significant differences among the brands?
  - How does the consumer judge the quality of a casual shoe?

Question

Outline a suitable research design for the above study.

Answer: Research is defined as a careful or critical enquiry or examination in seeking facts; diligent investigation in order to ascertain the fact. Decisions regarding that when, where, how much, by what means, concerning an inquiry or a research study constitute a research design. It is a research strategy. It constitutes the blue print for the collection, measurement and analysis of data. A marketing research design specifies the procedure for conducting and controlling the research project. The research design may be exploratory research study, descriptive research study, or hypothesis testing research study. The choice of particular research design would follow from the problem. The suitable research design for the present study is exploratory research design. It is appropriate for this formal leather shoe and casual shoe study. Because, it is flexible enough to provide an opportunity for considering different aspects of the preference of the customers towards casual shoe. An exploratory research will be effective and turnout to be fruitful if the following methods are adopted before the ignition:

1. Collection of primary and secondary data.
2. Survey of production and sale of formal leather shoe and casual shoe.
3. Experimental and control group study.
4. Treatment study/comparative impact study.

CASE NO. 19
INDIAN TOY INDUSTRY

The toy market in India is currently dominated by small unorganised sector, foreign made toys and the rest is occupied by the Indian made branded toys such as LEO or POLO toys, etc. Indian toys have not been able to compete in the international market because of their low quality and the safety standards of Indian toys are also generally poor. The Indian toy industry is nowhere in comparison to the toy industry in foreign countries. For instance, in USA, every year some thousands of new products are offered by hundreds of US firms three months before December. In contrast, Indian toy companies offer only about a hundred in one year. India has a great potential to increase production of quality toys to satisfy the growing needs of middle and upper class families. The market, currently, is so underdeveloped that it is difficult to predict the size of the untapped market in India. Marketing inputs are lacking and the trade is still dominated by wholesalers.

Competitive Scenario

There are currently over thousand toy manufacturers in the country belonging mostly to the unorganised sector. The organised sector consists of few companies who use some brand names (modern toys) for their toys and market them in cosmopolitan and big cities. While the unorganised/cottage sector products are usually low priced, their products are mostly sold even in small towns and villages. The market leaders in the organised sector are Leo toys promoted by Blow Plast Ltd., followed by Polo toys and new entrants being Funskool (India) Ltd., promoted by MRF Ltd., and Kidstuff. These companies prefer to go in for foreign collaborations as it obviates the need to design toys on their own for a market whose behaviour is uncertain. The volume of production in most of the units is not large enough to produce economies of scale and so the cost of production is high.

The target market for most of the firms is middle and upper income group. According to a research done by Funskool, most of the toys are for kids in the age group of 2-5 and a particular skew towards the male child. Both Leo and Polo and now Funskool have brought about a certain standardization in the toy industry. Most small manufacturers neither mention the price on the package nor the age group for which it is meant. Leo made up for its initial weakness in its product mix with a tie-up with Mattel, bringing in Barbie Doll for girls and Hot Wheels for infants. The manufacturers from the unorganised sector produce low priced toys with poor quality.

Questions

1. What would be the research objectives of this case?

Answer: To examine consumers purchase pattern of toys.

To ascertain consumers' opinion about toys and their views about branded toys.

2. What type of research design/information needed?

Answer

(i) Discern about branded versus unbranded toys.

(ii) Special features expected by the customers in a toy.

(iii) Consumers' awareness about the toy companies and brands.

(iv) Occasion and frequency of purchase of toys by the Indian customers.

3. What are the sources, nature and form of information needed in this study?

Answer

The purchasers must be interviewed with a structured questionnaire.

Information collected from the consumers belonging to different socio-economic segments is to be cross-classified to check whether opinions vary in different cross-section of the people.

4. State any two roles of unorganized sector producing toys in India?

Answer

(i) The unorganised sector caters the needs of low income people at low price.

(ii) The small manufactures compete with big manufactures with cheaper product.

5. Prepare a model questionnaire

Questions meant for the respondents

(Make a tick mark in the appropriate column/tell your answer)

1. Name of the consumer
2. Age of the consumer
3. Married/unmarried
4. Male/female
5. If married; Any child/No. of children
6. Age of child/children
7. Religion: Hindu/Muslim/Christian/any other
8. Community: FC/BC/MBC/SC/ST
9. Annual income of the consumer
10. Occupation of the consumer
11. When did you last buy a toy?
12. How frequently do you buy a toy?
    a. Once in a month b. Once in 3 months
    c. Once in 6 months d. Once in a year
13. Did you buy Indian toy or foreign toy? Indian Toy/Foreign Toy
14. If Indian toy, state the reason.
    a. Low price b. Comparatively good quality
    c. Fulfil our taste and culture
    d. Any other reason, specify....................
15. If foreign toy, state the reason.
    a. Good quality b. Durability
    c. Fulfil your expectation
    d. Any other reason, specify..................
16. Do you find Indian made toys to be good gift item to a child?

    Yes/No
17. If no, what are its defects?

    Specify.......................................
18. What was the price of toy you have purchased?
19. What is the general price range of toys you can afford?

20. When did you purchase the toy?
    a. During festival time b. During special occasions
    c. Birthday celebration d. Any other day, specify
21. Indicate below whether the following features are necessary, desirable or not:

Features	Necessary	Desirable	Not at all
Stimulating curiosity of the child			
Teaching child something			
Making pleasant sound			
Having musical sound			
Safe to play with			
Keep the child occupied			
Long-lasting			
Make the child confront a problem and solve it			
Have some movement			
Colourful			
Not poisonous if put into the mouth			
Not having sharp edges			
Imparting new ideas			
Having religious taste			
Cheap and best			
Good brand name			

22. Are you aware of the following companies:
    a. Leo-mattel Toys Ltd. b. Polo(Dinky) Toys Ltd.
    c. Kidstuff Toys Ltd. d. Funskool Toys (P) Ltd.
23. Are you aware of the following brands of toys? If so, tick
    i. Barbie doll ii. Machine guns
    iii. Mechano iv. He-man
    v. Jigsaw puzzle vi. Building block
    vii. Gi Joe viii. Any other specify
24. Say YES or NO
    * There is limited choice of toys in India
    * Toys available in India have limited educational value

* Buying a toy is basically wastage of money
* Variety toys should be low priced
* There is no much difference in toys.

CASE NO. 20
INDIAN PAINTS LIMITED (IPL)

IPL markets a wide range of decorative paints—of which synthetic enamel paints account for about 25 per cent of the company's turnover. IPL is presently manufacturing grade one synthetic enamel paints in a wide range of colours which are sold in 1 litre, 4 litre and 20 litre containers. IPL has a 16 per cent of market share of the bazaar sector for all synthetic enamel paints. The company's synthetic enamel paint is distributed nation-wide through four regional dealers in Mumbai, Kolkata, Delhi and Chennai, who supply the product to retailers in their region. The bazaar sector for synthetic enamel paint is highly competitive, complex and price conscious. The various brands of paints offered by the manufacturers have little difference amongst them and also brand awareness is low. IPL's existing brands are well established and the company would not like to sacrifice it, or change its market image.

To widen the market base for the company's products, it is planned to increase IPL's share of the bazaar sector for synthetic enamel paints from its present level of 16 per cent to 20 per cent in one year. IPL would like to consider the feasibility of product differentiation as a means of achieving the objective.

The company management felt that product differentiation could be done basically in three ways, i.e.,

(i) Range of colours: This is already very wide and hence offers little scope for further opportunity.

(ii) Size of containers: The present range of sizes offered is somewhat adequate: So this possibility was not given much attention.

(iii) Surface specific paints: It is felt that this area has the most scope for introducing product differentiation.

Consequently, the company management planned to produce a somewhat second grade paints which may be promoted for use on certain specific surfaces (like wood, metal, walls, etc.) and marketed at a slightly lower price than its existing grade-1, i.e. synthetic enamel paints. Since at the moment such surface specific paints were not offered by any of the competitors, it was felt that this special connotation may be encashed upon to develop a unique selling proposition. While its impact on the existing grade-1 synthetic enamel paints market will be marginal, it will, however, definitely affect the brands marketed by some of the competitors. In the long run, these competitors will possibly imitate this new idea. But, being first to introduce a new idea, the company expects to achieve its marketing objective (i.e., increase the market share) through evolving suitable promotion and trade discount policy and ultimately reap the advantage of an innovator.

While the production people are much aware of different attributes of surface specific paint, the decorative paint market is, however, somewhat unique. It consisted of two distinct types of end users, namely, civil contractors, furniture makers and garage owners who constitute the 'institutional segment', while household buyers formed another segment. But in the ultimate selection of brands by household sector, the labourers (i.e., the men who are involved in executing the painting job) and dealers play an important role. Under these circumstances the company management wished to gather more specific information about this market behaviour aspect.

Questions

1. What are the marketing research objectives that the company can initiate?

Answer:

(i) To study the reaction of end users about surface specific paint.

(ii) To ascertain the role of trade channel and other influencing agents.

2. What other set of alternative marketing research objective will you propose in the given situation?

Answer:

(i) To study the problems of labourers in executing the painting job.

(ii) To study the role of dealers for getting more specific information about market behaviour aspects in various market segments.

3. Define the specific underlying marketing issues and scope of each study.

Answer: There are many manufacturers offering various brands of paints. But they have little difference amongst them and their brand awareness is low. However, IPL has got product positioning and market image. But the company wants to widen the market base for its synthetic enamel paints and increase its share of the bazaar sector.

4. What are your explicit assumptions regarding the competitive scenario?

Answer: The company ventures to introduce product differentiation. Since the buyer sector for synthetic enamel paint is highly competitive, complex and price conscious, the explicit assumptions regarding the competitive scenario suggested are:

(i) Further varieties of colour.

(ii) Bigger, handy and reusable size of containers.

(iii) Certain surface specific paints like wood, metal, walls, etc., are introduced for reaching an increase in IPL's share at a lower price. Because such efforts are not taken by any other competitors in the market.

CASE NO. 21
GENERIC PROMOTION

Spice promotion in the United States takes many forms. To a certain degree, every firm which markets spices utilizes some type of promotion, but most of it is concerned with trade/ customer relations, in-store merchandising, local co-op advertising and sales support activities. The only consistent nationwide programme of promotion is that of the American Spice Trade Association (ASTA). This programme has been in continuous operation for more than 40 years, educating how to use them, and continually developing new taste-tempting ideas for seasoning food. In a land where a heavy use of seasonings is not a national heritage, the ASTA campaign strives to increase the frequency of spice usage, the variety of spices used and the degree to which they are used.

Meeting Challenges

Apart from promotion of spices *per se,* ASTA also promotes the image of the spice industry and its attention to quality control.

Solving communication crisis quickly—before they get out of hand—is another important part of rising spice prices. In 1979, the press began criticizing the spice industry for what they perceived as outrageously high prices. Headlines such as "If You Think Beef Is High Priced, Check Bay Leaves" become widespread. A challenge like that has to be met. At the same time, the answer must be carefully done. In general, the press is not interested in alibis or explanations from industry. Accusations make news; rebuttals do not. A positive answer which would have a good chance of being published is, therefore, to be devised.

It was frankly acknowledged that spices had risen considerably in price; hadn't everything? But, it was noted that a one-ounce tin of black pepper is enough to season an American's beloved breakfast eggs liberally for two years. A one-ounce jar of oregano is sufficient for 432 slices of pizza or 720 Italian meatballs. A 1-1/8 ounce container of cinnamon will improve 456 slices of Mom's apple pie.

Now, who would worry about a 50 cent price increase in products that do so much and go so far?

The press loved it. Simple, catchy facts and figures! Pretty soon the headlines were reading "Spices Are A Bargain", "A Little Spice Goes Along Way", and "Yield, Not Package Price, Best way to measure spices". The immediate mission was well accomplished.

ASTA's public relations programme was born of crises. In the 1930s spice consumption was on a steady decline. The medical profession, nutritionists and educators were advising against the use of such additives. New developments in transportation and modern refrigeration were giving Americans fresh, high-quality food. "Enjoy good food as nature intended-without additives", the experts urged.

ASTA decided it must counter with a strong public relations effort if the industry were to survive. Soon the recipes, photos began to flow to the press, telling consumers that spices made good food even better—that spices are the essence of creative cookery and good for the whole family. Included was research to allay the doctor's fears and education to convince the nutritionists that spices, properly used, could actually help them get people to eat foods that were best for them.

Such efforts, plus favourable conditions otherwise, have succeeded in completely reversing the attitude toward spices in the United States. From a postwar level of only 127 million pounds, USA has now (1980) moved to 460 million pounds in annual consumption. That includes domestic production as well as imports. And the upward trend continues to outstrip population gains today.

Opportunity for Producing Countries

There is still much needs to be done. Not all spices have matched the increases of the majority in the U.S. market. But the supplying countries should understand that ASTA's programme is primarily concerned with the overall use of spices and is not able to focus substantial activity on individual products. Strong promotion of a particular spice must remain the responsibility of the producers most involved. One example is the Vanilla programme which Madagascar has sponsored in the United States.

Natural Vanilla was a dying ingredient in the United States eight years ago, when Madagascar launched its programme. Artificially flavoured products were dominant and consumers were not conscious of the difference. But, Americans were beginning to be interested in natural products. So the campaign with the packaging symbol, called the Vanilla mark, designed to focus attention on those few special products that were still using real Vanilla, was started. This attractive mark reads "100% Real Vanilla" so that consumers do not have to search the fine print of ingredient listings. This is particularly helpful with ice-cream because manufacturers are not required to show ingredients on that product. Fortunately, Madagascar's initial promotional budgets were sufficient to make a fast start. The Vanillamark was not only eagerly accepted by the companies still using natural Vanilla; it soon happened that many other firms recognized its promotional potential and decided to switch back to the real flavour. At latest count, there are 260 licensed companies to display it on more than 700 products. Real Vanilla has won more attention than ever before in history.

Questions

1. Define 'advertising'.

Answer: The word 'advertising' originates from a Latin word 'advertire' which means to turn to. It may be defined as the process of buying sponsor-identified media space or time in order to promote a product or an idea. The American Marketing Association, Chicago, has defined advertising as 'any paid form of non-personal presentation or promotion of idea, goods or services, by an identified sponsor'.

2. Why and how does advertising for foreign markets differ from that for domestic markets?

Answer: Advertising for foreign market differs from domestic market in many respects. Multidimensional factors account for the differences in advertising for foreign market and for domestic market. The socio-economic factors, the political and legal factors, the religious factors and so many other non-economic factors like language account for wide differences in advertisement for foreign market and for domestic market. The business environment also differs from one continent to another continent and from one country to another country. The climate, the state of technology, taste and preference of the consumers and the custom, tradition, belief and value of the people too are responsible for heterogeneity in advertising. In most of the nations, advertisement is subject to control. For example, advertisement of alcoholic liquor and infant baby food is prohibited in India. In countries like Germany, product comparison advertisements and the use of superlatives like 'better', 'best', or 'excellent' in advertisement is not allowed. In the U.S.A., the Federal Trade Commission is empowered to ask for fuller disclosure of the relevant facts about products.

The distribution of income and wealth differs from region to region. Hence, the advertising strategy should differ between foreign market and domestic market. Differences in geographical conditions between markets may sometimes call for changes in advertising. Some countries protest for using ladies as models for anything and everything whether they use the product or not. For example, advertisement for the product of a US corn company would fail in Italy because Italians think of corn as pig food. Market is heterogeneous both in the supply and demand. New market segmentation technology has become an increasingly popular strategic technique in advertising. The Japanese culture provides for certain manners of dressing while the Indian culture provides for different patters.

Perhaps advertising is the side of international marketing with the greatest similarities from country to country throughout the world. Paradoxically, despite its many similarities, it may also be credited with the greatest number of unique problems in international marketing.

3. *State the part industrial trade fairs and trade centers play in international marketing of industrial goods.*

Answer: International marketing is defined as 'marketing carried on across national boundaries'. According to Hess and Cateora, international marketing is 'the performance of business activities that direct the flow of goods and services to consumers or users in more than one nation'. The industrial trade fairs and trade centres promote smooth flow of industrial goods and services to the users in the foreign market. Scarcities of industrial goods are minimized by the active role of trade fairs and trade centres.

4. *What are the various factors you will take into account in selecting an advertising agency for international advertising? Discuss the factors that are important in marketing organisational decisions for international advertising.*

Answer: One of the most important decisions an advertiser makes is selecting the agency for international advertising. There is no standard procedure for doing this. However, the following factors will be taken into account in selecting an advertising agency: Growth, experience, average age of service, manpower, agency's philosophy of business operation, campaign planning, agency's ability to create essentially good ideas, sales promotion, research, merchandising, agency's resources to produce or supervise production, the number and quality of the people, technique, availability of agency personnel for personal contact with the desired frequency, etc.

5. *Outline some of the major problems confronting an international advertiser.*

Answer: A unique aspect of advertising is the advertising agency. The first advertising agent was Volney B. Palmer who established an office in Philadelphia in 1841. The advertiser involves in the creative and media decisions. Some of the major problems confronting an international advertiser are: account conflict, division of functions and responsibilities between advertiser and agency, contradiction on both the client's and the agency's sides relating to advertising plans, etc.

6. *Enumerate the various techniques of sales promotion in overseas markets and state their suitability for promoting sales of engineering goods.*

Answer: Sales promotion has become increasingly important in inflationary times. When customers are watching their money, contests, special price promotions, point-of-purchase displays, and other action-oriented strategies can often be influential. Trade promotions, such as slotting allowances, allowances for featuring the product in retail advertising, display and merchandising allowances, and the like will promote the sales in the market. For promoting the sales of engineering goods, coupons, premiums, sweeptakes, low-cost financing deals, and rebates may be offered.

CASE NO. 22
EXPORT MARKETING

The trade in black pepper is unhappy that exports may not show a sign of revival in prices in the immediate future. World prices have been showing a downward trend for eighteen months and this has resulted in much lower earnings for exporters. The UK, West Germany and the Netherlands have cut their import requirements though the American demand has shown some growth. Brazil has been resorting to aggressive selling at lower prices and the expectations are that its exports will reach an all-time peak of 32,000 tonnes in the 1981-82 season. The 1981-82 Indian season is only about six weeks away. The Brazilian offensive has forced India to withdraw so to say from the US and West European markets and increase its reliance on communist buyers. As many as 14,500 tonnes of black pepper out of the 16,700 tonnes were shipped during 1980-81, the Soviet Union alone accounting for 12,647 tonnes. But exporters are concerned at the diversion on such a scale of this trade.

Q. *Had you been a pepper exporter, what would be your short-term and medium-term export marketing strategy in the above environment?*

Answer: Pepper is one of our traditional export-products. It is one of the spices (Cayenne pepper, pimento, nutmeg, mace, vanilla, ginger, cinnamon, cassia, etc. are other products coming under **Spices**).

Export means taking out of India any goods by land, sea, or air. "Export marketing is the performance of business activities that direct the flow of company's goods and services to the consumers or users in more than one nation"(Hess and Cateora).

The rate of growth of our black pepper export declined sharply in percentage terms.

The table below gives supports the above stated idea of India's spices export:

Year	Percentage share of spices export in the commodity groups
1991-92	1.5
1993-94	0.8
1995-96	0.7
1997-98	1.1
1998-99	1.2
1999-2000	1.0

India's major export markets

(percentage)

Country	1965-66	1993-94	1999-2000
USA	18.3	18.5	23.0
Japan	7.1	7.8	4.5
USSR	11.5	2.9*	2.6*
UK	18.1	6.2	5.9
Germany	2.2**	6.9	4.8

* Data for USSR refer to Russia only.
** Data for Germany refer to West Germany.

However, in terms of money value, our export of spices has gone up.

(Rs. Crores)

	1980-01	1990-91	1998-99	1999-00	2000-01	2001-02
Spices export	111	239	1633	1767	1619	1497

The trade in black pepper was not satisfactory because of downward trend in world prices and hence, our export earnings went down. Moreover, The UK, West Germany and the Netherlands cut their black pepper imports. Due to the aggressive and offensive policy of Brazil, India was forced to rely on communist consumers. However, there is an increase in the demand for our black pepper in the US market.

The Indian Government should give top priority for exports and draw up a plan for increasing the export of black pepper. I suggest an efficient sales and distribution organisation in the short-term and medium-term export marketing strategy/plan.

Indian Pepper Trade Association (IPTA) is to be formed for promoting the sale of pepper in the foreign markets. Every firm which markets pepper must concern with trade/customer relations, in-store merchandising and sales support activities. New taste tempting ideas and Indian Pepper Trade campaign have to be formulated to increase the frequency of pepper usage. People love attractive advertisement like: '100% Real Pepper', 'A Little Pepper Goes A Long Way', 'Enjoy good food as nature intended-without additives' "A one-ounce tin of black pepper is enough to season a foreigner's beloved breakfast eggs for two years" etc., Awareness should be created among the buyers that the peppers are the essence of creative cookery and good for the whole family. People should be convinced that pepper is not artificially flavoured product and eating of natural pepper is good for health.

CASE NO. 23
IMPORT PROCUREMENT
(Adapted from *Commerce,* Sept. 19, 1981, p. 527)

According to Rubber Board estimates, production of natural rubber in the country will be about 1.55 lakh tonnes in 1980 against 1.43 lakh tonnes in 1979. Demand for natural rubber during the year is estimated at 1.65 lakh tonnes—slightly lower than the 1.66 lakh tonnes in 1979. Thus, the gap between domestic demand and supply in 1980 would be 10,000 tonnes. The normal stock requirements of user units are around 56,000 tonnes on the basis of three months' average consumption. So, to bridge the gap between demand and supply as well as to provide a reasonable opening stock for the coming year, imports of 66,000 tonnes are necessary. Significantly, unlike in the past, this year growers and users seem to be agreed on the production and consumption estimates of the Rubber Board.

The Government has already authorised Central Purchasing Agency (CPA) to import 30,000 tonnes during 1980-81. However, hardly 500 tonnes have been imported so far. The delay in import is not due to any other extraneous factors. The Corporation has a long-term contract with the Malaysian Rubber Development Corporation for nearly one lakh tonnes of rubber, and of this 55,000 tonnes are yet to be imported. The hitch seems to be unsold stocks of imported rubber lying with the CPA.

CPA is reportedly holding around 5,000 tonnes of natural rubber which was imported last year. The quantity to be imported is decided on the basis of requirement registered with the Corporation by actual users, but even so till recently CPA was burdened with a stock of around 10,000 tonnes because allottees were not lifting stocks. As the tyre units have already taken delivery of the quantity intended for them, it is the non-tyre users who are refusing to lift stocks.

Rubber goods manufacturers have definite complaints about CPAs handling of imports, main among them being the substandard quality and the weight shortage of imported rubber. Moreover, the substantial margin between the prices of imported rubber and domestic rubber has made allottees prefer the latter, despite the earnest money of Rs. 1,000 per tonne deposited with CPA.

Indeed, as against the minimum control price of Rs. 8,250 a tonne, CPA's issue price was Rs. 12,990 a tonne. Average price of rubber in the Kottayam market during the whole of 1979 was below Rs. 10,000 per tonne. Domestic prices started to edge up from the beginning of the current year (1980), but even so the August average was lower than the prices fixed by CPA. According to the users, imported rubber has become costlier mainly on account of exorbitant carrying and other charges added by CPA to the landed cost. The industry claims that it can import its requirements at a much lower cost.

The Government has intervened by asking CPA to cut service charges by one per cent and to extend the bill marketing scheme from 45 days to 60 days. But the users still demand decanalisation of imports. They have even refused to register with CPA their future requirements of imports. Government meanwhile has insisted on the present stocks being cleared before considering fresh imports.

Speculation following the present deadlock has already started to push up domestic rubber prices. The average monthly price of lot rubber in the Kottayam market, for instance, has gained as much as Rs. 2,000 a tonne between June and August (from Rs. 10,480 to Rs. 12,490 a tonne). At present, at Kottayam, the RMA-1 grade fetches Rs. 13,650 a tonne compared to about Rs. 10,000 a year ago. The situation will be aggravated if this year's output falls below expectations owing to adverse weather, spread of plantation disease, etc.

The world rubber supply situation is not comfortable either, and world rubber prices are on the increase. During 1979 alone, Malaysian rubber prices increased by around 28 per cent. The uptrend is likely to continue because of the expected drop in Malaysia's rubber output this year. The skyrocketing of synthetic rubber prices, consequent on the crude oil hikes, would no doubt continue to lend considerable support to the natural rubber prices. Delay in effecting imports would thus ensure that the imports of rubber would be far costlier.

Questions

1. Analyse whether there is any case for decanalisation of rubber imports as demanded by the industry, or should the CPA be made more efficient?

Answer: There was a huge gap between domestic demand for rubber and supply of rubber. To bridge the gap, imports of rubber were necessary. The Government too authorized Central Purchasing Agency (CPA) to import rubber. The delay in the imports of rubber was not due the object to which it was attached or to what was being dealt with. The hitch seemed to be unsold stocks of imported rubber lying with the CPA because allottees were not lifting stocks. It was the non-tyre users who were refusing to lift stocks.

The problem was aggravated by the inefficient role of CPA. The CPA imported substandard quality and that too with shortage of weight. Moreover, the allottees preferred domestic rubber instead of imported rubber because the price of domestic rubber was lower than the imported rubber. It revealed the inefficiency of CPA in procuring quality rubber and containing the price of imported rubber. Hence, the Central Purchasing Agency (CPA) should be made more efficient.

2. What should CPA do with regard to finalization of import deals.

Answer: The rubber price in the domestic market was lower than the price fixed by the Central Purchasing Agency (CPA). Hence, the CPA should reduce the issue price by cutting the carrying, serving and other charges. The CPA should extend the Bill Marketing Scheme from 45 days to 60 days.

CASE NO. 24
TARIFFS AND SMUGGLING
(Extracted from the *Times of India*, May 9, 1984)

The present import policy (1984-85) for dry fruits has led to large-scale smuggling of dry fruits into the country and in turn is hurting the *bonafide* trade. Large quantities of dry fruits are stated to be smuggled into the country from Pakistan, where there is no import duty on these items.

Trade circles point out that smugglers have come to dominate the country's dry fruit trade during the past one year hurting not only the legitimate trade but also government. It is pointed out that the smuggling has been facilitated by the long common border between India and Pakistan which passes through Punjab, Rajasthan and Kutch. Nepal too has been importing dry fruits liberally through Kalkata Port, and a portion of these supplies are stated to be remaining behind in India. Passengers coming from abroad, particularly those arriving from Pakistan by land and from West Asia by air, are known to be bringing with them maximum possible quantities of dry fruits under the present baggage rules. Yet another source of supplies has been the larger and regular flow as gift parcels.

According to the Indo-Afghanistan Merchants' Chamber of Commerce and the Mumbai Kharek Bazar and Mewa Merchants' Association, the smuggled almond kernel from Iran is available freely at prices ranging from Rs. 100 to Rs. 125 per kg, when the cost of legitimate imports bearing the customs duty and other imposts works out to Rs. 190. Similarly, American almond kernel is being sold at Rs. 100 per kg. against the official cost of Rs. 150. The smuggled pistachio nut in shell is available at Rs. 130 and pistachio kernel at Rs. 140/150 per kg., against the landed cost of Rs. 170 and Rs. 210, respectively, of the products through trade channels.

The total customs duty on almond amounts to 190 per cent and that on other items to 140 per cent. The advantage to the smugglers is not limited to the heavy import duties, but they save on Central and State sales taxes and octroi duty, which together account for 10 to 12 per cent.

Trade circles have, therefore, been pleading that the import duty on dry fruits should be reduced to about 100 per cent, inclusive of the auxiliary duty. Such a step will reduce the profit in smuggling and can curb smuggling. The loss in revenue to the government can be compensated by raising the import quotas by 30 to 35 per cent. Such a rise in the import quota might increase the country's annual imports from Rs. 30 crores to about Rs. 40 crores, but it might be worthwhile since the country is already spending foreign exchange of this magnitude unofficially.

Q. Would you accept or reject the recommendations of the Trade? Give cogent arguments in favour of your decision.

Answer: Smuggling means conveying goods secretly i.e. importing or exporting goods illegally or without paying customs duty. The COFEPOSA (Conservation of Foreign Exchange and Preservation of Smuggling Activities) Act, 1974 empowers both Central and State Governments' officers to prevent smuggling of goods. The Smugglers and Foreign Exchange Manipulators (Forfeiture of Property) Act, 1976 provides for the forfeiture of illegally acquired properties of smugglers. But in practice, the above said Acts are not so effective in preventing smuggling.

Because of the loophole in the Import Policy (1984-85) and the baggage rules, large quantities of dry fruits were smuggled into India from Pakistan by land and from West Asia by air. The price of smuggled product was cheaper because of large scale evasion of customs duty, sales tax and octroi duty. Hence, I accept the recommendations of the Trade circles. The import duty on dry fruits should be reduced to 100 per cent. This will prevent smuggling. The loss due to this step can be compensated by raising the import quotas by 30 to 35 per cent. At the same time, home production should be increased in order to reduce heavy imports.

CASE NO. 25
IS ENTREPRENEURSHIP EDUCATION USEFUL?

For five dollars, you can own a "weather stone", one of several products being offered by a fifth-grade class at the Hunt School in Hunt, Texas. The stone is no more than a rock mounted on a small shingle that you put outside and watch. If the rock is wet, it's raining; if it's white on top, it may be snowing...and so on. The weather stone may be tongue-in-cheek product, but the entrepreneurship class for fifth graders is not. Fifth and sixth graders run concession stands, organise car parks for school events and have created several innovative board games. The class has been engaged in free enterprise education since 1983, earning as much as $240,000 a year from projects. Profits not only help underwrite new projects but also purchase new school equipment such as video machines and computers.

Entrepreneurship programs for youngsters, while applauded by many, are questioned by some educators who insist that they create mercenary instincts at the expense of fundamental education. Many children find that the stress of trying to run their own businesses is too much. Others find the reality of hard work to research, develop and sell something too much; they prefer to study in traditional ways. Still others find they are simply not cut out to pursue entrepreneurial careers. Those who support the programs point out, however, that these results are also important to give students a broader perspective on their own career aspirations.

Similar programs for grade school youth exist in dozens of cities across the United States, and more are being introduced. At the high school level, activity is often more pronounced. More than a hundred thousand high school students are involved in special programs and courses funded through state and local economic education agencies and foundations such as the Hugh O' Brien Youth Leadership Program. One program in the South Bronx area of New York focuses on disadvantaged youth. Founded by Steve Mariotti, the South Bronx project is designed to give inner-city youth an alternative to life on the streets. Mariotti's program brings students into seminars, takes them on tours through businesses, and introduces them to local entrepreneurs who have succeeded. Students also brainstorm a project, set up the business, and actively market a product or service. They are responsible for developing their own business plans and for succeeding or failing with their projects.

All youth programs have several things in common. They require students to develop their own ideas, plan ventures, develop their products or services for commercialization, and then go to market. They do their own market research, product design, licensing, venture administration, selling, and accounting. In many instances, they also must find financial backing. Advocates point out that students learn a wide variety of new skills through applications. They are introduced to bookkeeping systems, market research methods, planning systems, and economic processes. Mariotti claims that the most important aspect of his program is the "Psyche" value of becoming mentally stronger through personal involvement and self-directed activities.

Critics of these programs say that students may benefit from learning the mechanics of business, but the psychological redirection of effort toward making money is inappropriate. Young students, they say, should be out playing games and learning humanistic values; older students should be preparing themselves for careers. The controversy also involves the question whether entrepreneurship can be taught in the sense that most students simply do not have entrepreneurial personalities.

Questions

1. ***Discuss the concept of an entrepreneurial career and whether students can be taught to be entrepreneurs.***

Answer: Entrepreneurs are persons who initiate, organise, manage, and control the affairs of a business by effectively combining the factors of production for supplying goods and services in their chosen fields of activity, may be agriculture, small trade, industry, or even servicing. Students are resourceful and they possess enterprising qualities. The concept of entrepreneurial career can be explained and explored from the viewpoint of Economists, Sociologists and Psychologists. Economic incentives, social sanction and high needs for achievement drive people towards entrepreneurial activities. Students can be taught to be entrepreneurs on account of the fact that education, entrepreneurship, and economic development are interrelated. The present study found that majority of the entrepreneurs were either graduates or post-graduates, particularly in engineering and in other technical disciplines. It is also found that high level of education enables the entrepreneurs to exercise their talents more effectively and efficiently especially when there is a need to compete with others.

2. ***Based on what you have covered in this course, describe what you might envision as beneficial for grade school or high school students in courses similar to those in the case.***

Answer: Richard Cantillon was the first person to introduce the term 'entrepreneur' in management literature. A course which imparts the skill to bear uncertainty, take risk in career development and spirit of enterprise is one which I recommend for grade school students.

3. ***Take a position with respect to the controversy of whether to offer youth programs in entrepreneurship. Why would you support or oppose them?***

Answer: I extend my support for the offer of youth programs in entrepreneurship. Our country suffers from lack of entrepreneurial class. There is chronic unemployment problem. If we conduct programs for creating opportunities to become entrepreneurs, the country will have progress and prosperity.

CASE NO. 26
THE RAWSON SHOP

A women's specialty store dealing with a customer complaint.

The Rawson shop, a woman's ready to wear apparel store, catering to a medium and high-class clientele, was located in a prosperous, medium-sized eastern city. It was the only store in the area that had an exclusive to carry the original styles of Peter De Mose, a prominent Hollywood dress designer. De Mose originals, as they were called were priced from Rs. 1,000 for cocktail dresses to Rs. 2,500 for lavish silk evening gowns.

Then the original creations of all the foremost dress designers were displayed in the sprin, those manufactures of lesser quality dresses hurried to produce copies of these original. The copies sold for about one-third to one half of the price of the original creations and they moved very well in the medium and low class women's apparel stores. Almost every store that catered to both the medium and high-class trade carried the original dress as well as its copies because of the large profit resulting from the sale of a considerable number of these copies.

Miss David, owner of the Rawson shop, had recently encountered a difficult situation because of her policy of carrying both the originals and the copies of Mr. De Mose's creations. Mrs. Sturdevant St. Vanders prominent socialite in the community, had purchased one of Mr. De Mose's original cocktail dress for Rs. 1,000 ten days before the date that ten copies of this original were scheduled to arrive at the store. After three fittings within seven of the intervening days, Mrs. St. Vanders received her expertly altered dress.

Shortly thereafter at a party honouring her husband, Mrs. St. Vanders noticed that the wife of one of the young trainees in her husband's firm was wearing a cocktail dress that appeared to be identical to the De Mose originally that she was wearing herself. Mrs. St. Vanders introduced herself to the young woman and in the ensuing conversation she learnt that the young woman had purchased her dress at the Rawson Shop for only Rs. 400. Only a careful examination and comparison of the cloth of both dresses would have disclosed any difference in the two dresses.

The next morning Mrs. St. Vanders stormed into Miss David's office and demanded to know why she had been cheated. She said that she had worn the dress a dozen times in the past several months under the false assumption that she had the only dress of its kind in the area. Describing to Miss David her humiliating experience of the night before, she demanded her money back and threatened to cancel her account at the Rawson shop unless she was compensated to her satisfaction.

Miss David attempted to explain to Mrs. St. Vanders that her dress was the original of the particular creation but that there were many copies being worn because of manufacturing policies in the garment industry. Mrs. St. Vanders refused to accept this explanation and demanded a refund. Furthermore, she threatened to advise her wealthy friends to join her in refusing to patronize Miss David's store unless the Rawson shop discounted stocking copies.

Sixty per cent of the Rawson shops sales were made to middle-class purchasers. These customers, however, preferred the Rawson shop because of its reputation and of also catering to a high-class clientele. Miss David thought that she would lose her high-class clientele, unless she stopped selling the copies of Mr. De Mose's originals, yet she realised that 69 per cent of her customers would go for elsewhere to obtain the copies if she discontinued stocking them.

Summary of the case

The Rawson shop is a women's 'ready-mad' shop. Miss David is the owner of the shop. The shop sells the original high-class styles of Peter De Mose at high-price and its duplicates at low-price. One high-income customer by name Mrs. Vanders purchases original cocktail dress for Rs. 1,000. At a party, she notices one young low-income trainee of her husband's firm wearing the same type of cocktail dress. In the conversation, she learns that it was purchased for Rs. 400. She is annoyed with this. She quarrels with Miss David, demands her money back and threatens her with dare consequences.

Problems of the case

(i) Selling original dresses as well as their copies.

(ii) Lack of giving proper information and instructions to the customers.

(iii) Lack of customer awareness about branded quality apparel and their duplicates.

Question

1. If you were Miss David what would you do?

Answer: If I were Miss David, I would do following:

At the time of purchase, I will inform the customers about the original and duplicate copies of the apparels that are available in my shop. I shall make it a point to create awareness about branded high-quality/price wears and unbranded duplicates/copies which are substandard both in quality and price. I would say, at the time of purchase, that money will not be refunded at any cost on false complaints. However, exchange will be permitted if any defect is noticed before usage. If the customer is not informed about the features of popular brand and about the availability of their copies, then the shop-keeper is guilt of unethical practices and liable for prosecution.

2. Should she continue to carry both the original and the copies?

Answer: She shall continue to sell both the originals and their copies after giving proper warning about the substandard dresses. Customers should be well informed about the rules and regulations of the Shop. Originals and their copies should be separately displayed in different places in the same shop. Suppliers should be asked to have their own trade mark/brand name so as to avoid confusion among the customers. Because selling the duplicate garments without having distinguishable brand name or trade mark is unethical.

CASE NO. 27
RAMESH NAIL WORK

Mr. Ramesh was interested in investing in a small manufacturing activity. On enquiry, he found that there were no known manufacturers of shoe nail, that shoe nails were no "open general licence" for imports and that their annual imports amounted to about 1,000 tons.

Since nails were ¼ " and ½ " in length and 12 to 16 gauge in diameter, they were used in shoe making and to some extend in furniture making. Shoe nails could be made from coils and mild steel wire of the requisite gauge in two operations with the aid of an automatic nail making machine and a tempering machine to develop rust resistance. The cost of a well-known make of nail machine was Rs. 81,000, delivered and installed at the factory site. A tempering machine which could handle the output of four nail machines in a shift would cost Rs. 8,500 on similar terms. The normal life of nail making and tempering machines was 10 years. The machines would be worked at 80 per cent efficiency on a 24-hour basis. A semi-skilled machine could easily supervise the operations of 6 to 8 machines at a time with the help of a labourer. The capacity of nail machines was 500 nails per minute, 2,000 nails would weight 1 kg.

The mild steel wire required was made in India but not easily available. The cost of the imported wire was Rs. 12-46 per ton in port towns. Dependence on the imported wire would entail carrying stocks for 3 months operations.

Mr. Ramesh had two sites in his mind for the location of the new undertaking, i.e., port—town A and his home—town B. The location of the factory in town B would increase the cost of wire by Rs. 12.75 per ton. The operational and overhead costs for the two sites were estimated as follows:

	Town A (Rs.)	Town B (Rs.)
Daily wage rate of machines	22	20
Daily wage rate of labourers	22	20
Cost of power consumption per machine shift	8	6
Cost of packing stores, etc. per machine shift	8	6
Rent of factory per month	750	350
Administrative and selling expenses per month	1,500	1,500

The main wholesale market for the shoe nails was in Town A and the wholesaler's buying price was Rs. 184 per 100 kgs. The freight for nails from town B to town A was Rs. 10 per ton. Work-in-progress and stocks of finished products would entail locking up of 1 month cost of operations.

Mr. Ramesh was not interested in any project which earned less than 10 per cent on the capital invested. He was, therefore, wondering whether it would be advisable to invest in this project.

This is an introductory case in estimating financial requirements of a small enterprise. The issues that are related to determining the return on investment are:

(a) The best location of the unit.

(b) The minimum economic size of the unit.

(c) The amount of fixed and working capital required.

The candidates should be aware of the limitations of assumptions made by them in estimating the financial requirements.

CASE NO. 28
GOPU ENGINEERING WORKS

"What all we need is just Rs. 2,50,000 to solve our problem. We can make out own casting and stabilize out production" said Mr. Gopu, the managing partner of the Gopu Engineering Works which was a registered partnership firm started six years ago. Mr. Gopu, a non-technical man, looked after office work while his partner, Mr. Jogu had some experience in precision work. Jogu was in charge of production activity. The other odd repair jobs of the old firm (which they purchased) for some time before they came into contact with Mistry Engineering Co. Ltd., a well-known manufacturer of jeeps, trailers and tractors. Since the last six years Gopu had been doing exclusively Mistry's work, i.e., supply brake-drum equipment.

Production

A typical unit of brake-drum equipment included one drum, one plate, six grease retainers, 12 jeep plates (including shoes) and 10 hubs. Gopu works was working two shifts a day, the capacity for a shift being:

Drums	25
Plates	25
Grease retainers	30
Jeep plates	30
Hubs	15

The workshop worked six days a week. The equipment of the workshop included:

2	Lathes	Rs. 12,000 each (valued at the time of purchase)
3	Lathes	Rs. 10,000 each
1	Drilling machine	Rs. 1,200
1	Grinder	Rs. 1,900
1	Shaper	Rs. 700

The workshop consumed hand tools worth Rs. 5,000 each year. The office equipment was valued at Rs. 1,500.

Cost of Production

At two-shift capacity, the daily sales were around Rs. 400; the cost of raw materials consumed was Rs. 240. The monthly rent of office, workshop and godown was Rs. 100 monthly. The company paid Rs. 54 annually toward municipal licence and factory inspection. The maintenance of the two cars involved a monthly expenditure of Rs. 400. Mistry Engineering company used to send its own trucks to the workshop to take delivery of the drum equipment.

There were five lathe operators who were paid Rs. 5 each daily. The other five helpers who did odd jobs were paid a daily wages of Rs. 2.50 each. Payments were settled on a monthly basis. Most of the workers used to take advances from the company.

Asked how they determined the price of break-drums, Gopu, said, "The cost of castings is the price at which we buy them from our suppliers. We can easily determine the cost of machining them by visual examination. Our partner Mr. Jogu can tell you the machine hours required for a particular type of drum by just looking at it."

Of the five lathes in operation, two were in perfect condition. All the lathes could, however, be used for a variety of purpose such as all types of machining work, wood work, textile machinery parts and small gears.

Sales, Suppliers and Customers

The yearly sales for the first four years were around Rs. 1,70,000. In 1978 and 1979 they were Rs. 1,60,000 and

Rs. 1,40,000 respectively. The fall in sales volume was due to shortage of raw castings. In 1979 they had to refuse an order valued at Rs. 60,000 from Mistry's for want of adequate supply of castings. It was for this reason alone that they had been operating two shifts only. For some time, Gopu Works purchased the castings from Rama Engineering Works. As Rama Engineering Works stopped supplying castings to Gopu Works owing to pressure of work, they switched over to Industrial Motors Ltd., who, despite their heavy demand for castings required for their product-line, obliged Gopu Works by supplying them a limited quantity of castings. Commencing on their connections with Industrial Motors Ltd., Jogu said, "It is really very kind of them to accommodate us. God bless them!" In 1977, when the Industrial Motors had an unused capacity of castings, Jogu took advantage of that by placing of order for brake-drum parts (hubs, drums and plates—1,500 units each) valued at Rs. 1,00,000. He thought, he could store the parts for some time and thereby overcome his problem of scarcity of raw castings. Since he had neither money nor war house space, he could not take immediate delivery of the parts. He promised to take delivery of them as early as possible. Meanwhile, the Government's ban on import of tractors had seriously affected the break-drum requirements of Mistry's with the result the Gopu Works had to suffer production setback. Mistry's switched over to production of trailers which were required by military department. But the plates required for this trailers were different from those which Gopu Works had recently purchased from Industrial Motors. Though Gopu Works could use some of the parts (hubs and drums) it took almost two years to liquidate half to the huge inventory purchased from Industrial Motors. In October 1979, an inventory of parts worth Rs. 5,000 stocked in his own godowns. Asked why such huge inventory was still lying with him in a period when there was scarcity of raw material, Gopu said, "the castings we have in our godown are not the ones we require today. The type of castings we need changes with the shifts in the product-line of Mistry's". Gopu also revealed that before undertakings Mistry's work, they did for some time the work of trailers for Das Ltd., but had to discontinue it for want of the particular casting required for the work. He was, however, confident of the continued patronage of Mistrys as they were expanding by manufacturing truck trailers. He said, "Looking to our long-standing cordial relations with Mistry's we will be able to get some sort of ancillary type of work which you known every big factory has to depend upon the small scale industry."

Commenting on the future plans of Gopu Engineering Works, Gopu observed, "Naturally, we have to find new field of work and since we have got good experience in this particular line, we would like to mass produce this equipment (break-drum) so as to meet the requirements of Indian automobile market. In order to achieve this, we must have our own foundry and some modern automatic machines in order to withstand competition. The foundry will ensure as regular flow of casting to feed our machinery. Besides the break-drum equipment, we would also like to manufacture some small tool machinery because my partner Mr. Jogu has had some experience in that line also. If we start our own foundry, we would be able to sell our castings to Mistry Engineering Works and a number of other large Engineering concerns. We have been studying the demand and supply of these casting for the last three years.

There is a great demand for quality castings. As regards quality, we hope Rama Engineering Works would help us they used to do when we bought our casting from them. Besides, we can always consult the Small Industries Service Institutes for necessary technical advice.

Mr. Gopu estimated that an investment of Rs. 2,50,000 will be required for the following:

	Rs.
1. Cupola	75,000
2. Land	25,000
3. Raw material inventory	50,000
4. Machinery and tools	1,00,000

The capacity of the proposed foundry would be 100 tons a month. Gopu said that a ton of casting would sell at Rs. 1,500 while the cost of raw material per ton would sell at Rs. 700. Every 100 tons of good casting would require casting of 150 tons of raw material.

Gopu and Jogu had private savings amounting to Rs. 30,000. Besides they jointly owned a house valued at Rs. 1,25,000. They did not have any other property.

Questions

1. Estimate the financial requirements for running a foundry as desired by Gopu.
2. What are the sources of financing the foundry?
3. What are the problems likely to be encountered by Gopu in selecting up his own foundry?
4. How do you appraise the management of Gopu Works?
5. What suggestions would you like to make to Mr. Gopu in managing his enterprise?

CASE NO. 29
WTO AND INDIA—MILLENNIUM BUDBEAR

Industry is unprepared as tariff and investment issues hot up at WTO.

When you're getting ready for the school boards, it can be upsetting to be told that you have to take the university examination instead. This can be specially disconcerting if the curriculum includes subjects that are known to be tough or tricky to handle.

India and most of the developing nations are finding themselves in a similar situation as the developed world tries to broaden the agenda of trade liberalisation in what is termed the Millennium Round.

The Millennium Round is meant to be a comprehensive single undertaking that the European Union and Japan are hoping will be kicked off the World Trade Organisation (WTO) ministerial meeting at Seattle. On their checklist are contentious new subjects like a multilateral framework on investment, global competition and the opening up of government procurement to international scrutiny, in addition to the built-in agenda of old issues at the WTO. The most volatile of the new issues is the framework on investment that would enshrine the rights of multinational corporations (MNCs) in a binding agreement, giving them the same rights as domestic firms.

India is baulking at the enlargement of the agenda. Its contention is that the Uruguay Round of negotiation that led to the formation of the WTC in 1994 dealt primarily with issues of interest to the industrialised countries and had not led to much gain for the Third World. It wants a detailed assessment of the impact of this round—it includes a total of 29 agreements apart from 25 ministerial declarations and undertakings—before a new round of trade talks is launched. Says Commerce Minister Ramakrishna Hegde: "The very idea of a new round frightens many of us since we are yet to recover from the hangover of the Uruguay Round."

Much of the disenchantment of the Third World stems from its inability to have gained market access, specially for textiles and agricultural exports, and the refusal of the rich to implement the special and differential provisions for developing countries. In short, the concessions have been marginal compared to the obligations imposed on them. Which is exactly why the world needs a new round, says Leon Brittan, the caretaker European Commission's vice-president who has emerged as the strongest champion of the Millennium Round. Brittan who has been wooing 'difficult' Asian governments to win support for his pet project, points out that no country is really happy with the Uruguay Round. Therefore, a broader, liberalized agenda in a comprehensive round of negotiations would take care of everyone's grips. "Any issue or area of concern to any WTO member can be put forward for inclusion on the agenda, which is agreed upon by consensus," says Brittan in his typical hardsell. Undoubtedly, a comprehensive round has its plus points: it allows members to gain advantage in one sector by making concessions in another. Liberalisation is holding out for sectoral negotiations not least because comprehensive negotiations take far too long—the Uruguay Round took seven years to conclude—while the EU is pushing the point that a catch-all-round would spread the benefits more evenly. Indian officials remain skeptical.

They say that apart from the iniquitous fallout of the Uruguay Round, three agreements of critical interest to the country are coming up for review in 2000—agriculture, services and TRIPs (Trade-related Intellectual Property Rights), New Delhi. As the major economic powers pursue their different agendas, India is drumming up support for a review of how earlier agreements have worked. It has managed to get the backing of the other members of the SAARC that the focus at Seattle should be unbiased appraisal of the impact of trade agreements on developing economies. Besides, says Nripender Nath Khanna, special secretary, WTO, in the commerce ministry: "There is a tremendous amount of work to be done to meet our obligations under Trips and Trims." True enough because the legal and administrative backlog is pretty daunting. But the underlying concern is that India and other developing countries should not be made to pay twice over for the same concessions. For instance, the special and differential treatment for such countries has never been implemented simply because these are not clearly defined and are not enforceable. "The imbalance has to be redressed now and not as part of a new package," says Khanna.

He is also firm that certain misconceptions have to be laid bare on industrial tariffs, in particular. Although the industrialised world has brought down tariffs to an average of 3.8 per cent post-Uruguay, the figure conceals a high level of peak tariffs. Around 20 per cent of US tariff peaks exceed 30 per cent while nearly a quarter of those in the EU and Japan exceed 30 per cent. Worse, the effective rate of protection in the US doubles between leather and footwear; in Japan it zooms from 66 per cent to a very high 200 per cent.

The focus is on tariffs because commerce ministry officials believe it's the most significant of the issues that will be raised. India, whose tariffs are still high—the weighted average is 30 per cent against and lower 12 per cent in Southeast Asia—will come under pressure to bind all tariffs (only 62 per cent of the total tariff lines in the manufacturing sector are bound now) and to cut them. Former Commerce Secretary A.V. Ganesan, who played a pivotal role in the Uruguay Round, says India's problem on this score is different from other developing countries since we still have not come out of the quantitative restrictions regime.

To prepare the blueprint on tariffs the government needs close and continuous input from industry, and this simply is not forthcoming. Not one of the apex industry organisations—CII, FICCI or ASSOCHAM—has made its concerns clear. An exasperated Khanna complains: "I find it disturbing that five years after the Uruguay Round, I am asked to conduct awareness workshops by the CII Industry is not discharging its responsibilities. What we need is a professional response from industry—industry- specific and knowledge-specific—on the issues of concern to it."

Sadly, there were no replies from any of the apex industry organisations. A committee member confides that as a result what was produced was a thin report of little value. "In the absence of a feedback from industry we were shadow boxing," says Ganesan.

That is always the case with Indian Industry, laments Biswajit Dhar, senior fellow at the New Delhi-based research and consultancy organisation Research and Information System (for the non-aligned and other developing countries). Barring a few sections like pharmaceuticals and automobiles which are waking up to the challenges, industry has not articulated what it wants, he says, whereas in the developed world the entire negotiating mandate is decided by the manufacturing sector and the farm lobbies.

There are other potential minefields. The West's attempt to introduce transparency and end discrimination in government procurement could end a comfortable cushion of protection for domestic industry. If buying by government is brought under WTO regulations, the price advantage of 15-30 per cent will end as will the practice of giving them contracts. What exactly is at stake? No figure of the total procurement is available but the

Directorate-General of Civil Supplies and Disposals, the central purchasing organisation, alone tots up to a bill of Rs. 3,500 crore annually. This, according to official estimates, is only a small part of the government's huge procurement expenditure. Yet, industry has remained somnolent in the face of challenges.

Ganesan's wake-up call is a mandatory WTO audit for every company. The trade negotiations guru says every company should be in a position to say if it can meet the challenge of imports. If not, it should understand what its shortcomings are. Instead of bleating for high tariff barriers, industry has to learn that the response to the WTO is part of the larger issue of globalisation. And it's not the WTO but technological changes that are driving the new wave of globalisation. Is industry listening?

CASE NO. 30
BIG BANG
(*The New Indian Express*, April 28, 2008)

Indian-born steel tycoon Lakshmi Mittal is the richest man in Europe with his fortune estimated at a staggering 27.7 billion pounds, even as he emerged as Britan's wealthiest person for fourth year in a row. Over all, the steel baron, whose wealth saw a whopping increase of 8.5 billion pounds in a year, is the sixth richest in the world, a rich-list published by the *Sunday Times* said on Sunday. His company Arcelor Mittal is now worth more than 57.2 billion pounds and the Mittal family's 43 per cent stake is worth 24.6 billion pounds.

According to the list, the Ambani brothers, Mukesh and Anil, although they have parted ways, together were rated as the richest in the world at a combined worth of 43 bn pounds, ahead of America'a Walton family, owners of Wal-Mart (38.4 bn) and Microsoft chief Bill Gates (29 bn pounds). Then were two more Indian entries in the list of 50 richest in the world in 2008—K.P. Singh (property—15 bn pounds) and Shashi and Ravi (steel, oil, telecoms—7.5 bn pounds).

Meanwhile, the Hinduja Brothers, S.P. Hinduja and G.P. Hinduja, Chairman and President, respectively of the group were Britain's second richest with 6.2 billion pounds. Leading NRI entrepreneur Lord Swaraj Paul was the fourth among the ten richest Asians in Britain, the list said.

The London-based Caparo Group of 77-year-old Lord Paul, British Ambassador for Overseas Business, is making hefty investments in the booming Indian economy. In 2006, its profits were 55 million pounds on 660 million pounds sales.

CASE NO. 31
THE MINISTER'S MASTERSTROKE*

Our dynamic and far-sighted Finance Minister Mr. P. Chidambaram has called for a global action on prices. He has called for a global consensus on tackling the spiralling prices of food and oil across the world and warned against its turning into a global contagion. We wholeheartedly support the minister's exhortation. If we could make foreigners solve our problem, what could be better than that? Unkind critics have criticised or ridiculed him for looking to others, when action should have come from himself. But that is because they do not realise the innate logic, if not ethics, behind the minister's masterstroke.

As champions of *aam admi,* we have always considered Mr. Chidambaram to be the most likeable minister in the UPA Government. We liked his song and dance about nine per cent GDP growth which would have gone up and up to 12 per cent but for the U.S. sub-prime crisis.

We also liked his irrational exuberance when the benchmark BSE Sensex crossed 21,000. Market analysts, rating agencies, brokers were all confident that the Sensex will cross 30,000 by end of 2008! We thanked God that we had a pro-market Finance Minister who wants Indian companies to go on a global acquisition spree.

When global funds flooded Indian share market and the rupee began to strengthen against the mighty US dollar, our cup of joy just overflowed. India's growth story was blown out of proportion. Having edited the country's most

* (Corporate India, April 30, 2008)

influential economic newspaper for a day, what is wrong if Mr. Chidambaram thought India is going to buy several Fortune 500 companies?

India has been praised by no lesser person than Nissan Motor's chief for its "frugal engineering skill..." Tata Motors produced a car costing Rs. 1 lakh—a fantastic feat which was thought impossible by other global car makers. Nano enhanced the brand value of India! So what if these achievements made the Finance Minister a bit dizzy? He dreamed consolidation of Indian banks and making Mumbai a global financial centre. India's forex kitty had crossed $300 billion and Reserve Bank was worried about flood of dollars inflow.

Credit disbursal for industries soared. Remittances from Indians working abroad touched a new high of over $30 billion. Everybody treated India as a special investment destination. The Government's "incredible India" campaign swelled tourists to the country putting pressure on hotel rooms. However, the minister made a small slip. It never occurred to him that all these plus points were incidental to the global bull cycle which was bound to end at some points of time. Our learned Finance Minister erred. We thought well, it is only human to err!

Being a strong supporter of globalisation, he thought, inflation is dead and gone. Money is freely flowing as borders are vanishing. If a country is poor, it can always look at foreign funds. Apart from FIIs, there are private equities, sovereign funds—all eyeing India for investments being the second fastest-growing nation in the world.

For nearly four years, annual inflation rate was less than 5 per cent. RBI said it was manageable below 5 per cent. The Finance Minister wanted the industry to fire on all cylinders. After the economy achieved 9 per cent GDP growth, he was keen on a double-digit growth rate. The architect of the "Dream Budget" saw potential for growth in every corner.

Then came like bolt from blue US sub-prime crisis. But hopes continued. Like others, he believed crisis in the U.S. was not going to affect India. India's growth is almost self-sustaining.

Overall exports to U.S. and imports from U.S. are negligible. India is decoupled.

They say misfortune does not come singly. The U.S. sub-prime crisis dried up FII inflow. Indian stocks collapsed. Credit to industry declined. And worse, inflation raised its ugly head. Mr. Chidambaram was dumbfounded. But being practical, he gave top priority to curb inflation. Along with price rise came shortage of essentials.

This then is the logic and the ethics of Mr. Chidambaram's call for global action against price rise. The causes are global, the consequences are global, the remedy, per force, has to be global.

It is another matter that other countries are too busy fighting their own war on inflation. Mr. Chidambaram has done his duty. He can no longer be blamed for high prices. If others do not respond to his sagacious call, what can he do?

Cheers to Mr. Chidambaram. We wish him a long tenure as Finance Minister.

This is in lighter vein but should we just laugh it off...?